RESCUE

Also by Peter Selby:

Look for the Living (SCM 1976)
BeLonging (SPCK 1991)
A World Come of Age (SPCK and Cowley 1983)

RESCUE

*Jesus and Salvation
Today*

Peter Selby

First published 1995
SPCK
Holy Trinity Church
Marylebone Road
London
NW1 4DU

British Library Cataloguing in Publication Data

A catalogue record for this book is available
from the British Library.

ISBN 0–281–04897–5

Typeset by Datix International Limited,
Bungay, Suffolk
Printed in Great Britain by Biddles Ltd.,
Guildford and King's Lynn

Contents

ACKNOWLEDGEMENTS

This book is a revision of lectures given to the Vacation Term in Biblical Study at St Anne's College, Oxford, in July 1994. I am very grateful to the Committee of the Vacation Term for the honour of the invitation and the stimulus it provided, as also to those whose questions and comments about the lectures assisted me in the process of clarification and revision.

My colleague Dr Stephen Barton gave me the necessary encouragement to undertake this enterprise, and then read chapters 2–5 in draft. His careful criticisms enabled me to make some important improvements, and I am very thankful that I had the benefit of his support and perception as the work proceeded. Ms Rachel Boulding of SPCK offered invaluable comments on the draft, and I very much appreciate her invitation to make the lectures into a book and the care she has taken with the project.

That I have been able to undertake this task is due to the generosity of the William Leech Foundation in enabling my appointment to a professorial fellowship in the Theology Department of the University of Durham. I am deeply appreciative of the opportunity this affords. During the period when the lectures were in preparation I was also privileged to be a member of the Church of England's Doctrine Commission which was considering the doctrine of salvation; I am most grateful to my fellow-members for the stimulus of our meetings and conversations.

Peter Selby
Durham

1

Who Needs
Rescue?

OUR EYES AND ears are assailed on every side with situations demanding rescue. This is not to say that the world is a wretched place, a vale of tears in which all we can hope for is to survive. It is to say that our wonder at the beauty and potential of the world around us constantly yields to a sense of sadness or outrage at all that threatens and overshadows us: the sufferings of people and communities, so often apparently arbitrary, and the cruelty with which people's claim on their share of the resources of the world is denied. Instead of responsible contributors to the shared life of humanity, we see people reduced to being victims, dependent suppliants in an unequal struggle against their circumstances. The sights and sounds of such denial cry out for rescue.

There is, however, a large gap between hearing the cry and making an adequate diagnosis, let alone a prescription of the rescue that is required. How is sickness to be cured or poverty eliminated? Are we to locate blame, and if so where? Is there, apart from the specific ills by which people are afflicted, some more general ill, some dislocation in the life of the world? Is there, in other words, some general rescue that is required if all the more particular distresses we see around us are to be remedied?

At the centre of the Christian enterprise lies a promise of rescue, and a person whom God sent and named as Saviour. To understand more adequately what Jesus offers in the way of rescue and how we are to appropriate that offer is the aim of this book. Yet immediately we express the theme in these terms we encounter some of the central problems about the credibility of the Christian gospel in the modern world. For the language in which the Church has expressed its diagnosis, its understanding of what it is about the human situation that requires rescue, has in large measure become distant, even abstract. In appearance and meaning it has become largely limited to the religious sphere of life. In that respect our context is vastly different from that which confronted the Church in the period of the New Testament. What we see there is the believing community addressing clear-cut and specific cases of the need for rescue, cases not only of needs which we recognize as religious, but those where people need delivering from physical, mental and material constraints too. Consider this example:

> One day Peter and John were going up to the temple at the hour of prayer, at three o'clock in the afternoon. And a man lame from birth was being carried in. People would lay him daily at the gate of the temple called the Beautiful Gate so that he could ask for alms from those entering the temple. When he saw Peter and John about to go into the temple, he asked them for alms. Peter looked intently at him, as did John, and said, 'Look at us.' And he fixed his attention on them, expecting to receive something from them. But Peter said, 'I have no silver or gold, but what I have I give you; in the name of Jesus Christ of Nazareth, stand up and walk.' And he took him by the hand and raised him up, and immediately his feet and ankles were made strong. Jumping up, he stood and began to walk, and he entered the temple with them, walking and leaping and praising God.
>
> Acts 3.1–8

Nobody can envy a person who is paralysed; but we do sometimes wish that our need of rescue were as clear as his was. When your need is obvious and inescapable, the nature of the rescue you require is also obvious. When we lie on a bed of sickness racked with pain, there is not much doubt about what we need: an end to it soon, if possible instantly. In such a situation we do not take kindly to being told about the value of pain as a survival mechanism, let alone the ennobling effect of suffering. We want deliverance, and we want it fast.

One difficulty in spending time thinking theologically about salvation and talking about it is that we cannot put out of our minds the fact that there are millions of people out there whose situation presents us with just such urgency. We live in a world in which that is not some occasional awareness that strikes us, but one that clamours constantly for our attention, propelled into our living rooms with every news programme and documentary. It is hard to see how the refugee families of Rwanda are going to be assisted by our efforts to grow in understanding of the complexity of the biblical language about salvation, and the way in which ideas about it have developed in subsequent periods of church history. With so much urgent distress about, what purpose is served by knowing of the centuries of controversy about how Christ saves us? Or how, we may ask, does it help those in such great need to know that there are millions who have found rescue in the name of Jesus? It is easy enough to reflect that we 'do not live by bread alone' when we are not in the midst of a famine.

When we hear the word 'salvation' we often do not think of such things. When Christians profess that Jesus Christ came down from heaven 'for us and for our salvation' they may think of the world's religious needs, its sin, its labouring under the threat of meaninglessness or the fear of death, and perhaps even its tendency to conflict and war. We are unlikely to find ourselves thinking of people's being saved from immediate physical needs: did the Son of God come to feed the hungry? Or to heal the sick? These were, of course, among the gifts and graces which he brought; but when we think of salvation we think of something more religious, more mysterious, than any of these things.

So we can describe the difficulty that lies in the background of this book in two ways. On the one hand we see those of our fellow human beings who do not seem to have any particular distress from which to be saved; on the other, those in the gravest distress seem to require succour of a far more direct kind than 'salvation'. On the one hand, the message of salvation seems to address needs which many of our contemporaries do not feel they have; on the other, it seems to bypass the most pressing needs of those asking for rescue.

Yet the Scriptures do not encourage us to see salvation in these mysterious, or religious, or rather abstract terms. They are not coy about the fact that armies were 'saved' from defeat or that slaves were saved from bondage. Salvation included blind people receiving their sight, deaf people hearing and hungry people being fed. Salvation meant many things, and there seemed to be no need to distinguish various 'aspects' of salvation from each other by giving them different names. At the root of the meaning of the word lies the idea of 'spaciousness', and that spaciousness stands for all the freedoms into which people need to be delivered and the overcoming of all that constrains them from entering into those freedoms. Life has many kinds of constraint from which people need release into the open space of God's good purpose: constraints of economic privation, political oppression, disability and the social disadvantage and sometimes stigma that attach to it, destructive relationships, supremely of abuse and violence. There are constraints upon persons, and constraints upon whole peoples and communities: military invasions and occupations; the economic oppression brought about by distorted terms of trade which make it impossible for some nations to take their full part in the community of humankind.

These are the realities from which rescue is required, and the Scriptures are full of examples of such things. They also contain many stories of the deliverance God has achieved for people from those constraints. In the Bible salvation, rescue, is not just a hope or a heartfelt longing: it is a reality, experienced in the life of God's people. What is more, God's people only exist by virtue of its having been saved.

What launched the Hebrew tribes into their distinctive faith was an experience of the impact of rescue: the religion of the Old Testament sprang out of the Exodus from Egypt. God had kept a promise. God had saved. God could be trusted.[1]

That is a vital point to be clear about at the outset: the people whose story, laws, literature and exploits are recorded in the Bible did not see themselves as like other peoples whose stories have been chronicled, people who happened to inhabit a particular country or derive from a particular ancestry. Occasionally they did think of themselves in that way, as a kinship group, or a group based on some shared merit or achievement; then they could indeed be as exclusive and nationalistic as any other nation.

Sometimes the protection of their territory or the insights of their faith demanded that they act in this way. But often such behaving 'like other nations' derived from a fatal religious error, the error St Paul calls 'boasting'. His objection to it is not what ours might be – that it is bad manners or tiresome or self-assertive – but that it makes a fundamental error about the character of God's people. Their existence, and this is true of the people of the New Covenant just as much as it is true of the people of the Old, was entirely due to a saving act: they were made by being saved, and that was what they had to remind themselves about every time they brought the produce of the land to present to the Lord:

When the priest takes the basket [of firstfruits] from your hand and sets it down before the altar of the Lord your God, you shall make this response before the Lord your God: 'A wandering Aramean was my ancestor; he went down into Egypt and lived there as an alien, few in number, and there he became a great nation, mighty and populous. When the Egyptians treated us harshly and

5

afflicted us, by imposing hard labour on us, we cried to the Lord, the God of our ancestors; the Lord heard our voice and saw our affliction, our toil and our oppression. The Lord brought us out of Egypt with a mighty hand and an outstretched arm, with a terrifying display of power, and with signs and wonders; and he brought us into this place, and gave us this land, a land flowing with milk and honey.

Deuteronomy 26.5–9

From constraint into spaciousness, from slavery to freedom, was their journey, and they were always to remember what they had been, slaves in Egypt. Therefore they were a people that existed only by virtue of God's saving action. This is what the people of the New Covenant also had to remember, as St Paul reminded them.

So with us, while we were minors, we were enslaved to the elemental spirits of the world. But when the fullness of time had come, God sent his Son, born of a woman, born under the law, in order to redeem those who were under the law, so that we might receive adoption as children. And because you are children, God has sent the Spirit of his Son into our hearts, crying 'Abba! Father!' So you are no longer a slave but a child, and if a child then also an heir, through God.

Galatians 4.3–7

The name of the Messiah, Jesus, 'who will save his people from their sins', about which we shall be reflecting further in the next chapter, is in that sense the only name a Messiah could have, one who would reconstitute the community on the original basis of its existence, the basis of having been saved. The movement he founded was in fact a community of those who had need of salvation, who had been 'outside' and were brought 'inside' by his life and his offering of himself.

Christians hear these words and often make a kind of translation of them, one that confines their reference to the spiritual, making the 'slavery' a religious one, a metaphor; and it is easy to suppose that is how it was from the beginning. But metaphors are not just the inventions of people who are good with words; they have to connect, if they are to do their work, with the experience on which they are based. For example, if white westerners are to continue to use the metaphor of slavery, they have to face the fact that even at the level of folk memory they have very little concept of what slavery was like. If you are going to use it you have to give a little history lesson to start with, in a way that would be much less necessary in a Caribbean community, for instance, where the popular memory of slavery and its significance would still be around. What that means is that the biblical metaphors that occur in the gospel of salvation – the freeing of slaves, the remission of debts, the offering of an acceptable sacrifice – all had power in the earliest Christian community because they referred to experiences people could see all around them. What is more, they were not, therefore, 'mere' metaphors; they also had a literal content: Jesus had come to declare release to captives, sight to the blind and good news to the poor.

As well as the need to retain our hold on the historical content of the gospel of rescue, there is another challenge too: it lies in the fact that saving people into God's spacious realm is not something which happens free of cost. It may indeed be a realm with room enough for everyone, but that does not prevent the resentment that arises in the mind of those who reckoned they had a prior claim on that space, because they owned it, held it as of right, had earned it or whatever. So we find that, where people are saved, the hearts of others are hardened. As people were released from the constraints from which they needed deliverance, so others found in those events a threat not just to their own position but also to much that they held dear. Salvation was an event, but it was also a lesson.

That lesson is hard: saving people is like paying one-hour

workers the same as twelve-hour workers; and the backlash against the welfare state, against supposed 'scroungers' and 'queue-jumpers', is reminder enough of the reaction that brings about. It is like welcoming back with delight and rejoicing an offspring who has wasted the family's goods and good name, and we know what that can do to a family. It is like demanding that people remember, when they are faced with a debtor unable to repay them, that they enjoy their economic prosperity only because they themselves have not had some pretty massive debts called in. How much chance is there that the world economy is about to be reorganized on that basis, even though the rescue of vast numbers of the world's people from starvation may require it? And most of us do not readily remember, when we feel someone is indebted to us, the size of our own debts.

So the gospel of rescue emerged into a world where there were some clear situations requiring rescue, and where that rescue could be related to the history of a people that knew itself to have experienced rescue at the hands of a God who saves. That connection, between people's need of salvation and the character of God revealed in their history of salvation, was constantly being pressed home in the preaching of Jesus and the Church. That meant in turn requiring people who might resent the rescue of others to face hard questions. We know that the act of requiring that was itself costly: the passion of Jesus Christ and the persecution and martyrdom of many Christians were directly attributable to the unwillingness of individuals and communities to make way for those whom God was saving. They did not see themselves as in need of rescue, and saw no reason to allow their perceptions, their way of life, their structures and their presuppositions to be changed for the sake of those who did. 'Who needs rescue?' is the question implicit in much of Jesus' action and preaching: he had come for the sick, the blind, the unrighteous; but *who* were the sick, the blind and the unrighteous? – that was the question his audience were constantly asked to face.

But there were other hard aspects to the gospel of rescue. People can present their needs without recognizing their deeper roots, and what they would have to give up if they were to have those needs met. Such was the young man who asked Jesus,

'Good Teacher, what must I do to inherit eternal life?' Jesus said to him, 'Why do you call me good? No one is good but God alone. You know the commandments: "You shall not murder; You shall not commit adultery; You shall not steal; You shall not bear false witness; You shall not defraud; Honour your father and mother."' He said to him, 'Teacher, I have kept all these since my youth.' Jesus, looking at him, loved him and said, 'You lack one thing; go, sell what you own, and give the money to the poor, and you will have treasure in heaven; then come, follow me.' When he heard this he was shocked and went away grieving, for he had many possessions.

Mark 10.17–22

Knowing that something is wrong, that all is not well, is one thing; desiring the full implications of change is quite another. It is for that reason that Jesus is recorded as constantly requiring people to consider what it is they really want. 'Do you want to be made well?' he asks the man at the pool of Bethesda (John 5.6), as though there might be some doubt. Indeed there would have been; for the position of suffering victim has its distinct attractions, and the possibility of losing that position can appear very alarming. 'What do you want me to do for you?' he asks Bartimaeus (Mark 10.51), as though it might not be obvious. The offer of rescue has, however, to be grasped, and carries all kinds of implications of the loss of one's previous status. The story of the rich young man occurs immediately after the episode of Jesus' rebuking the disciples for their unwelcoming attitude to the children who were being brought to him, commanding them to let them come; 'for it is to such as these that the kingdom

9

of heaven belongs. Truly I tell you, whoever does not receive the kingdom of God as a little child will never enter it' (Mark 10.14, 15). The willingness to abandon status – whether it is that of the person enjoying high regard or the one accustomed to a life of exclusion – is the necessary condition of rescue.

The offer of rescue is therefore, and has been from the beginning, a challenging confrontation with existing realities. It offers to the marginalized the chance of entry into the abundant life of God's realm, but at the same time requires of them a willingness to take responsibility for their life and their choices. It is not rescue as the image often presents itself to us, the lifting of a helpless person down to the ground in the arms of a strong fireman or the bringing to shore of a drowning person by an energetic and competent lifeguard. It is an invitation into freedom and responsibility, and that is why the record tells us that it was an offer declined by many.

On the other hand, rescue is also offered to those who appear in their own mind to be quite well placed in the existing order. The healthy, the righteous and the powerful are also offered what they do not know they need. They are told that their rescue lies in accepting what they would rather not have: the company, as brothers and sisters, of all those whom they had previously been able to brand as belonging outside. The world was to be turned not so much upside down as inside out: 'None of those originally invited shall taste of my supper', says the host, determined that his house should be filled with guests (Luke 14.23, 24). The exclusion and the inclusion turn out to be indissolubly connected: if God's large space is to be peopled, then those who seek to possess it as their own will have to take their place on the outside. It is not that the space of God's generosity has suddenly become narrow and constricted. Rather, that if the only basis on which you are prepared to inhabit God's realm is the exclusion of others, then you will discover that you are in fact to be on the outside, and that the one who came to call sinners to repentance did not come for you.

These motifs that surround the New Testament's offer of salvation are crucially important, though not of course the only ones that could have been selected from the full range of biblical material. In considering the rescue God offers we are faced with something that is rich in meaning. At the same time in many ways that meaning is ambivalent. The gospel of rescue aroused in those who received that rescue a sense of release, dynamism and hope. It also produced among those convinced they were the 'saved' recourse to pride and patterns of rejection as destructive as any they had themselves encountered in the days when they or their ancestors were among the excluded. Those who have wanted to could use Jesus' words and actions, and the preaching and life of the early Church, to justify exclusive attitudes. Sometimes indeed the survival of the Church as an institution depended on their doing so. It has not been different in succeeding ages. Yet as will appear, presenting the gospel of rescue as fundamentally aimed at the inclusion of the excluded is in no way unfair to the constant theme of the Church's original proclamation.

What is clear is that what Jesus said became what his key followers then believed to be the basis of their life together in Christ. That was understood as on the one hand welcoming and healing to those held down by disabling disease and excluding attitudes, and on the other hand subversive of the authority and status of those who saw themselves as on the inside. What is clear also is that such teaching, and the actions which were seen to flow from it, were found to endanger the social fabric, and to merit persecution and often death.

This presents us immediately with major difficulties in our appropriation of the gospel of rescue. We do not in fact find ourselves in a situation where repeating the message of Jesus and the apostles places us in any danger. We find that that language has been, for as long as we can remember, effectively translated into concepts that belong to the realm of religion. They offer to those burdened by a sense of guilt the possibility of forgiveness; they offer to those who find life purposeless the possibility of a new sense of direction and meaning; they present to those facing the fundamental human joys, of birth and love, a language for their praise and delight; they offer to those facing the archetypal human catastrophes, death and tragedy, a sense of being included in a love strong enough and eternal enough to sustain them. But in the process of that translation of the gospel of salvation into concepts that belong to the realm of religion, something else happens as well: the gospel does not turn the world inside out, but on the contrary lets the world continue much as before. It does not give seats at the table of honour to those least respected, but on the contrary invites them to believe that what really counts, the rescue God really offers, is a sense of meaning and forgiveness they can receive just as well without changing anything. Dietrich Bonhoeffer raised the question whether the gospel could be translated into a world where religious needs of the kind I have been describing could not be assumed to exist, where the meaning and power of the gospel had to be rediscovered in non-religious terms. His challenge is critical, not least because the gospel of rescue was also a powerful instrument of change, and needs to appear as such today.

Two examples in current debate in this country can serve to focus questions about how we see salvation, and in particular how we recover its essential dynamic. First is the issue of our living in a world of many faiths and a nation of many faiths. That has been seen to present real difficulties for a traditional view of God's rescue as having been accomplished in Jesus Christ, whose status as Saviour has been professed by the Church as ultimate, final, decisive. His was the only name under heaven by which we could be saved. The message to Muslims, Hindus, Sikhs, Buddhists and Jews seems all too clear: it is that they stand effectively in the same place as those who have no religion and see no need of one. The latter do not seek religious answers to questions of meaning, while the former seek such answers and have found wrong ones.

But does this not assume that the gospel functions in a world which is in the grip of a religious competition? Must it not mean that the Church is a stallholder in the marketplace of spiritual meanings, trying to attract customers to be interested in our wares, glad in a way that there are other stalls selling other products because that increases the interest, but hopeful that in the end the customers will make the right choice? We have to ask ourselves what is the relationship between that view of the world and of religion within it, and the central Christian proclamation of rescue for all. Is not that view of the world as a backdrop for a competitive market in religion one of the things we need rescue from?

That is not to say that we are excused from a serious engagement with specifically Christian faith and practice, with the teaching of Jesus and the way in which he was proclaimed. Nor is it to say that in our commitment to what Jesus has offered and the Church has proclaimed in worship and witness we shall not from time to time find ourselves in conflict with the adherents of other faiths, and indeed other ideologies too. But it is saying that any way of dealing with our relations with other faiths which puts us permanently on the inside, the winners or the market-leaders in a competition in religion, threatens in principle to undermine our grasp of the very things we claim to be proclaiming. In a group that was discussing the relation between Christian and other views of salvation, one member remarked with passion, 'I don't know about that; but I do know that the adherents of other faiths where I live don't feel owned.' Clearly he believed he was saying something about some of the first steps that needed to be taken if they, and we, were to be saved.

My second example is the debate that seems to have arisen yet again about whether it is a good thing for the particular relationship of the Church of England to the state and the sovereign to continue. It is not an issue of very pressing interest in itself, principally because it turns out to be a contest in which vastly exaggerated claims are made on both sides. Altering some of the mechanisms which operate at the top of the Church and state so as to loosen the links a bit will do very little to alter the relationship between the gospel and the people of our land. It will do very little to overcome the alienation of the Church of England from the poorest people of England or from those who have seen the Church as part of their problem rather than part of their solution. So the claims of those seeking change seem to be grandiose. On the other hand, those who defend the way things are by referring to the great value of our links with the powerful need to face the question, great value *for whom*? And when they go on to be concerned lest any modification of the present arrangements would send 'wrong signals', we need again to ask, wrong signals *to whom*? Are we thereby stating that our real interest in the gospel of salvation lies in its ability to speak to those who are already included within the structures that reward certain people with power and prestige? And what then is our relationship to the gospel proclaimed by the one who said that what he was rescuing us into was a place where dinner invitations were sent to those least likely to ask you back, and money would be lent to those unlikely to be able to repay?

Such are some of the issues which come upon us when we engage with the gospel of salvation. But there is always a further sense of threat that arises at this point: is this all a politicizing of the gospel, something which will reduce its scope and deprive it of its capacity to speak to those central issues of human life that may not be political but are crucially important to the lives of people? We do still need to hear Christ speaking to us in relation to our dying, to our sense of sin, to our struggles when we have them with a loss of meaning. The man at the Beautiful Gate with whom we began did have personal needs, whatever we may also see and learn from the conflict that was aroused by his healing. The message of rescue may turn the world inside out, may set in train conflicts and debates and reversals of the order of things. But does not Christ speak to us in our moment of need, and must we always have in mind those issues of community transformation which represent such a source of disturbance to us? Does not Christ speak to us in our moments of personal need?

Indeed so; but the Christ who offers rescue at deathbeds, to penitent sinners, to those facing meaninglessness, does so because those are also moments when, whoever we are and have been in our social position, we are placed on the outside, needing to be included. Those are precisely the moments when the word we need to hear is a gospel that insists that (as Peter said in his explanation of the healing of the crippled man at the Beautiful Gate) 'it is not by our own piety that we have made this man walk'. For this assures us that it is 'through the faith of Jesus' that we have been able to renew our strength, to walk and not faint. The Bible insists that such a word has been spoken and lived; the rescue we are offered is both to hear that word and not to place burdens on others that will prevent them from hearing that word and receiving the rescue which it promises.

2

The Name

JESUS IS SAVIOUR. So he is called and so, in the faith of Christians, he turned out to be. For the people of Jesus' world, it could be no surprise that persons should turn out as their names suggest; that was in a way only to be expected. Behind the naming of Jesus lies a long tradition that attaches a great significance to the names people have, especially if they are the names which God gives them. Even more significant than that, however, is the fact that Jesus belongs to the people which believed that it uniquely had been given the divine name: God had caused the divine name to dwell among them; they were called by God's name, and during the periods when they were able to worship God in the temple at Jerusalem, it was the place where God had placed God's name.

Yet we must not suppose that a culture which attached such importance to the name of God and the names of people is a culture totally foreign to us. Before we look at the power of Jesus' name and its background in the significance of names and naming in the Bible, we need to reflect that in our world also something of the power and significance of names continues to be part of our life and experience. God's name and the name of God's people may have been revered as the revelation our forebears knew themselves to have received; but we too experience names and naming as central to our humanity. Our names are part of our personality and are the source as well as the sign of our dignity and uniqueness. They are not just 'labels' for us, and we do well first to consider the way in which names work in our own culture before we examine their special meaning for those who shared Jesus' Jewish faith and who came to acknowledge him as the Saviour God had chosen and named.

NAMES AS WE KNOW THEM

'Without wishing to mention any names . . .' Such words are seldom the beginning of a purely neutral utterance. Something is about to be said that is not to somebody's credit, or that might cause somebody embarrassment, and everybody knows it. Keeping names secret is generally what we do in situations where there is danger around or the potential for it, or where for whatever reason we do not wish to draw undue attention to a person's identity.

So those engaged in any kind of professional relationship with others, who wish to share with a wider audience the discoveries they are making, take care to conceal names and anything else that will reveal identities. If people are to reveal, and struggle with, their personal difficulties, they will only do so when they are assured of confidentiality: even if some general learning is to be shared with a wider audience, we need a pledge of anonymity. In such situations we need to know that we shall be *'nameless'*.

If the concealment of names is something we do for our protection, that certainly lends itself to abuse as well. People in positions of power whom we should wish to see accountable for their actions keep their identity secret and thereby avoid the finger of blame. Often as a result the truth of situations is never grasped, and a general unease is left because the person responsible is never 'named'.

Yet if the naming of names is very much associated with the darker side of life and the revealing of unpleasant truths, we know that is not the whole story. Naming names can also be a means of bestowing credit, of honouring achievement or courage. Rolls of honour and certificates of achievement are inscribed with names. War memorials list not merely the numbers but the names of those killed in action; passers-by may not know who those concerned were, but with the list of names goes the sense that those who lost their lives were unique, were related to others in their family or circle of friends. Books bear their authors' names, and by that means declare not only responsibility for the contents but also to whom credit is due in subsequent reference or quotation.

At the most intimate level, the choice of a name for a newborn infant is among the most intimate and carefully undertaken of all parental acts: parents-to-be often keep the 'short list' of names very private; whom a child is named after can be no small matter in the dynamics of a family. If a baby is stillborn, parents testify to the importance of being allowed to bury the infant by name, and they are unlikely to use the same name for a subsequent child. The name at that point confers a particular person's identity, unique to that individual, not to be shared with another. What is more, as the child grows towards adulthood, the name can be a particular source of concern and a sign of personal responsibility. Is the name to be abbreviated, and if so how? Is a nickname received as a sign of affection, often held privately within the family or peer group who alone are allowed to use it? Or are such nicknames a means of teasing, part of a playground culture that in adult life we remember with considerable pain as the time when we were constantly being 'called names'? We all know people who have deliberately changed their name or asked to be called by a particular name or abbreviation; they bear witness to the fact that it is very important to make your name your own. It is part of what characterizes you, and the character it confers has to be right.

Addressing and being addressed by name is something we all know to be of the first importance. To be recognized by name after many years is not just a sign of an admirable skill on the part of the person doing the recognizing: the experience contains the sense of being singled out, of being given importance. Conversely, we feel awkward about asking a person's name, or being unable to introduce them by name, when we feel their name is one we should know. The embarrassment signals the sense that the absence of a name may demean or insult someone. It is for that reason that while 'I am hopeless at remembering names' may be received as a confession or a piece of modesty, such statements can also make us uneasy because we can come to suspect that the comment may be an excuse. Is this really a problem of memory, we ask ourselves, or does it represent a deeper failure to be aware of other people and to honour their individuality?

Controversies about names also signal wider and more serious contention. The Holy Land, Palestine and Israel are names for overlapping geographical entities; but the diversity of names also signals the contention there is about whose land it is and who should govern it and for what purpose. Derry and Londonderry are the same place, but then again they are not: the bricks and mortar, streets and open spaces may be the same, but the identity of the city is bound up with unresolved conflict and deep community loyalties.

The contention may not always be violent, but it is significant nonetheless: 'Will you be taking your husband's name?', addressed to a woman on the verge of being married, signals the large and unresolved agenda of issues in the relationship of women and men. It is a question that is not avoidable, and the answer to it declares a stance, a loyalty, a position in an argument. The fact that the question used not to arise marks out our time from earlier ones.

Such, in very brief terms, is some of our experience of our name, and the names of the persons and places we care about. Enough has been said to suggest that our name is no small matter to us, but is very close to the heart of our being. We may be a collection, even a unique collection, of physical and mental characteristics, but attaching to that collection our name brings them effectively to life. Our brown hair and short temper, our talent for writing short stories and our weakness for strong peppermints are all redeemed from the realm of the hypothetical and the fictional. They are brought to life, as it were, by the fact that they belong to a person who can be called by a name, and who belongs to a group, a

family, a community, a nation, all of which in their turn can
be named.

EXPERIENCE AND SCRIPTURE

These experiences of the power of names are ones which we
take with us into any discussion of the role of names, and of
the power of Jesus' name, as they confront us in the New
Testament record. That record is full of careful attention to
names: names are given, and then names are changed. Some of
those names are filled with an ancient historic significance, or
have meanings which indicate the kind of person someone is
meant to be and the destiny that awaits them. Some examples
of this concern with names will be attended to shortly. What
is important to establish at this point is that we approach the
significance of the names that fill the pages of the New
Testament, and the meaning which the New Testament
writers ascribe to those names, on the basis of our experience.
We are not in this matter to be dominated by a merely
historical concern with what those names meant then, and
how writers then handled them. We do not approach the
New Testament communities simply as a visiting anthropolo-
gist might approach a previously unknown tribe. We are not
mere visitors concerned to know about our forebears' customs
and way of life. We can at the same time assume a common
human experience that might include both ourselves who
read the text and the earliest Christian communities about
whom we are reading.

We have of course to acknowledge how much we have
learnt from those who have undertaken such 'visits' to the
New Testament, bringing to it their sociological and historical
skills. Such visits have had an enormous value in clarifying
the particular circumstances which lie behind the documents
as we have them. In just the same way the investigations of
archaeologists and textual critics in an earlier generation were
the main source of critical knowledge of the Bible. But if in
that sense we always look at the texts from the outside we

may do inadequate justice to the fact that we for our part are bound together, in two mutually enriching ways, with those whose faith has been handed on to us in the text as we have it.

First, to state the obvious, the Scriptures were in fact produced by people, and that remains true whatever the particular theory of inspiration that any of us may hold. They were, naturally, people of a particular time and place, responding to and formed by movements of history, both great and small, which were unique to their time. To know that history gives us some insight into the New Testament authors and those others whose conversations, sermons, letters and stories lie behind them. We can in that way glean a little more of what it was that led them to express themselves as they did.

Yet human beings are not simply the product of particular places and times, isolated from all other places and times. They do not remain completely opaque to us until we acquire a detailed understanding of their history. For they are also and significantly *human*, flesh of our flesh and bone of our bone, endowed with a range of capacities and life experiences that belong to human beings at all times and places. We are able therefore to engage with them and relate to them at least to some extent, knowing that even if their times were remote from ours and the events that shaped them different from those that have shaped us, there is also a community of interest and a continuity of human living. That must enable us to form some relationship to those whose thoughts and lives we read about in the Scriptures. So, to take our current concern, while there are clear signs of the way in which history and culture affected the significance of names in biblical times, we are united to our biblical forebears by sharing the same quest for identity and significance in our lives which our names represent for us.

The second way in which we are related to those who gave us the Bible works in the other direction: if we bring to our examination of biblical texts and characters our sense and experience of what it is to be human, they bring to us their crucial role in forming us in faith and life. Their faith has given rise to our faith and, to refer again to our current concern, we are united with them by sharing with them our participation in the name of Christ, the identity that is given to people whose lives are committed to the following of Jesus.

To state that such a connection exists is not, of course, to be clear yet what form it takes. We have yet to consider how our forebears' concerns inform ours, or how their expression of faith should determine ours. But we must acknowledge that connection as an essential component in our interest in and approach to any biblical material. We read Scripture out of faith, expecting to encounter faith. We have been moulded in our faith by those whose faith we encounter in the Bible. At the same time, we expect that our experiences of faith and life will illuminate and deepen our understanding of what our forebears have to tell us.

Specifically, we expect to encounter those who had experience of the power of the saving name, and who had found themselves given a new name, a changed identity, in the light of their experience of the following of Jesus. In him they had recognized God's rescue, their own need of it and experience of it, and had seen therefore a way that could lead to life rather than death for the world. We bring to our encounter with them all the occasions of rescue of which we have been aware, and all the longing for it that we perceive. We expect in that encounter to learn something new that will change and enrich our own perceptions. We know at the same time that, without those perceptions and questions which caused us to be concerned to study Scripture in the first place, the stories, teaching and wisdom of the New Testament would make no sense to us.

So we have reason to expect that it will be possible to move back and forth between experiences in our own lives and our encounters with the New Testament. We expect that such a movement will surely change our perception of both, each illuminating the other. It is a movement in which all kinds of 'expertise' will make their presence felt: the knowledge of the historical and social background of the text, and the professional disciplines of (for instance) psychology or sociology, which have in so many ways revolutionized our understanding of life in our time. More than that: those kinds of human knowing which are not called 'expertise' at all, but which are the common currency of human living, our everyday way of seeing things, will have an indispensable part to play in our way of engaging with the New Testament.

Such a movement between experience and text is not some purely modern invention, foreign to the New Testament. Its writers, after all, brought to their experience of Jesus and of the life of the Church all that they had learnt of God and seen recorded about God's care for Israel. So the authority they experienced as operative through the name of Jesus reflected the immense reverence which they felt towards the Name of Yahweh. God's identity is revealed, and then surrounded with awe; God's Name is given to Moses, and thus God's very being is tied up with the fate of a particular people. God's Name, repeated in such songs of liberation as Moses' triumph song (Exodus 15.1–18) comes to stand for all that distinguishes Yahweh from the gods of Egypt, and therefore later from the gods of the surrounding culture. God's Name speaks in itself of the radical freedom for which God's people have been rescued. As Brueggemann says, it is 'a new name that redefines all social perceptions'; it is

> the very name of freedom which Egypt couldn't tolerate and the freedom slaves could not anticipate. The speaking of the name already provides a place in which an alternative community can live. So prophets might reflect on the name of God, on what his name is, on what it means, on where it can be spoken, and by whom it might be spoken. There is something direct and primitive about the name in these most primal songs of faith and freedom.[1]

God's Name is for that reason on no account to be 'taken in

vain', used for purposes alien to the being and character of God. So grave was the risk of such taking in vain that piety came to forbid the use of God's Name at all. Yet that Name lived in the Jerusalem temple and in the ongoing story of God's own people.[2]

So a vast wealth of tradition would have been accessible to the first hearers of the Church's preaching, informing the attitudes which they brought to any use of the name of Jesus, and at the same time changing in important ways their concept of God's Name and the power of it. The name of Jesus, like the Name of God, was powerful to heal and save; the name of Jesus, like the Name of God, indwelt God's people. Yet the name of Jesus was available to be spoken for the carrying out of his work, and so God could be known as present among God's people in a new and intimate way. So the movement between text and experience that we undertake in a very conscious way, in the period since the Scriptures have been subjected to various different kinds of criticism, has always in effect been a feature of the life of the believing community, even if the process was not acknowledged as such.

There is a graphic illustration of this movement back and forth between present experience and biblical record at the opening of Edward Schillebeeckx' three-volume statement of Christian faith and life, where he begins his 'experiment in christology' with 'The Story of a Crippled Man':

> We have all seen him, have we not? Day after day, always at the same old pitch, more or less unnoticed by people in a hurry, who still, sometimes with an air of boredom or surprise, sometimes with a friendly nod, will toss him a coin as they go on their way. There he squats in his small corner, alone, the familiar figure of the local crock. So has it ever been. 'And a man lame from birth was being carried, whom they laid daily at that gate of the temple which is called Beautiful to ask alms of those who entered the

temple.' (Acts 3.2) Came the day when Peter, one of the Nazarene's following, noticed him sitting there. There was some exchange of words between them. The next thing people saw was their neighbourhood cripple fully restored and walking as well as anyone.[3]

The telling of this story is intended to engage the reader's interest; but we should not understand that as a mere device drawn from the world of advertising where products are linked with sunshine or sex to make them seem more desirable. In this case the connection is essential to the enterprise of reading Scripture or living the life of faith. In approaching the story of the man lying by the Beautiful Gate through the experience of encountering people in similar circumstances today, our imagination is engaged so that we expect the story to influence our faith and our discipleship. Conversely, if in our day we approach those who are oppressed by disability and deprivation in the light of the story of the man at the Beautiful Gate, we find that our responses are changed and our heart is opened to new possibilities of generosity and solidarity.

THE SAVING POWER OF THE NAME
What is more, this particular story is not merely a general illustration of the way in which we are to approach scriptural material. The story is also precisely the starting point we need in our search for a contemporary understanding of what is meant by the saving power of the name of Jesus. Immediately after the event to which Schillebeeckx refers, we read the account of Peter's explanation: 'And by faith in his name, his name itself has made this man strong, whom you see and know; and the faith that is through Jesus has given him this perfect health in the presence of all of you' (Acts 3.16). Then, at the point where Peter is being interrogated about the healing of the lame man, he makes the same point again:

25

Then Peter, filled with the Holy Spirit, said to them, 'Rulers of the people and elders, if we are questioned today because of a good deed done to someone who was sick and are asked how this man has been healed, let it be known to all of you, and to all the people of Israel, that this man is standing before you in good health by the name of Jesus Christ of Nazareth, whom you crucified, whom God raised from the dead. This Jesus is "the stone that was rejected by you, the builders; it has become the cornerstone." There is salvation in no other name under heaven given among mortals by which we must be saved.'

Acts 4.8–12

The lesson is not lost on their interrogators, even though they do not in the least like what they have heard: 'What will we do with them? For it is obvious to all who live in Jerusalem that a notable sign has been done through them; we cannot deny it. But to keep it from spreading further among the people, let us warn them to speak no more to anybody in this name' (Acts 4.16–17). The actions of the Jerusalem authorities in relation to Peter and his friends in banning the use of the name of Jesus parallel the decisions of tyrannies down the ages who have recognized that, if subversion of their power was to be prevented, they had to stop the opposition finding a name around which people could coalesce in a movement for change. It is not that a name functions as a kind of magic word, a spell which can be made to produce a desired effect if you simply get it right. Rather, what we see here is the power of the act of naming to bring into action as a coherent whole all the capacities of the subject being named. The memories, actions and qualities of the one being named literally come to life with a new capacity to command loyalty and to exercise their strength. That is why a name can be powerful and, for those who oppose what it stands for, dangerous.

This reality of the power of naming appears prominently in

the New Testament, and one very obvious place is at the very start of Luke's narrative, where it is clear that the choice of names is an integral part of the events that are being set in train. The first annunciation, and the one that is importantly rejected, is to Zechariah. He is told that Elizabeth will bear a son, and that he is to be called 'Yahweh-has-shown-favour', John. The name fits the event, the birth of a child out of time, as well as the destiny that child is to fulfil: 'Even before his birth he will be filled with the Holy Spirit. He will turn many of the people of Israel to the Lord their God. With the spirit and power of Elijah he will go before him, to turn the hearts of parents to their children, and the disobedient to the wisdom of the righteous, to make ready a people prepared for the Lord' (Luke 1.16, 17).

Zechariah rejects the promise, representing in action what the Fourth Gospel states in more general terms, that 'The Word came to his own and his own did not receive him' (John 1.11). As a result, the angel says that he is to be deprived of the power of speech 'until this has happened'. What emerges clearly, after the account of the angel's announcement to Mary, and her visit to Elizabeth, is that what has to happen for Zechariah to receive back his power of speech is not just the birth of John but also his *naming*:

Now the time came for Elizabeth to give birth, and she bore a son. Her neighbours and relatives heard that the Lord had shown his great mercy to her, and they rejoiced with her. On the eighth day they came to circumcise the child, and they were going to name him Zechariah after his father. But his mother said, 'No; he is to be called John.' They said to her, 'None of your relatives has this name.' Then they began motioning to his father to find out what name he wanted to give him. He asked for a writing tablet, and wrote, 'His name is John.' And all of them were amazed. Immediately his mouth was opened and his tongue freed, and he began to speak, praising God. Fear came over

27

all their neighbours, and all these things were talked about throughout the entire hill country of Judaea. All who heard them pondered them and said, 'What then will this child become?' For, indeed, the hand of the Lord was with him.

Luke 1.57–66

The events surrounding the naming of John capture themes that are going to be of crucial importance for the rest of the story of God's saving work. In the birth of this child 'Yahweh has shown favour', a graciousness rejected by a man who is representative of the devotion of the temple cult. Elizabeth names the child correctly with a name that is not 'after his father', one by which 'no one in his family is called'. So John, 'Yahweh-has-shown-favour', takes his place in the story of God's action towards God's people. It is the story of how the graciousness of God comes to transcend ties of kinship and blood and is bestowed upon those who respond faithfully, even those who had dwelt in darkness outside the realm of grace before. In assenting to that name for his son, Zechariah is rescued from the consequences of his rejection, his speech restored in a song of praise (Luke 1.67–79) in which he specifically acknowledges John's place in the story of the rescue of God's people:

'And you, child, will be called the prophet of the Most High, for you will go before the Lord to prepare his ways, to give knowledge of salvation to his people for the remission of their sins. By the tender mercy of our God the dawn from on high will break upon us, to give light to those who sit in darkness and in the shadow of death, to guide our feet into the way of peace.'

Luke 1.76–9

All are to share in the experience of rescue first described with a direct simplicity by Elizabeth: 'This is what the Lord has done for me when he looked favourably on me and took away the disgrace I have endured among my people' (Luke

1.25). Thus from the beginning 'Yahweh-has-shown-favour' is the preparation for the story of the rescue of God's people by the person of God's appointment, Jesus, 'Yahweh-has-saved'.

This is the name which, in the New Testament, is seen to bring with it all the power of God. As happened in the case of John, the name is similarly a part of the announcement of the impending birth (Luke 1.31–4), and it is Matthew who makes its significance clear in his account of Joseph's dream:

> Now the birth of Jesus the Messiah took place in this way. When his mother Mary had been engaged to Joseph, but before they lived together, she was found to be with child from the Holy Spirit. Her husband Joseph, being a righteous man and unwilling to expose her to public disgrace, planned to dismiss her quietly. But just when he had resolved to do this, an angel of the Lord appeared to him in a dream and said, 'Joseph, son of David, do not be afraid to take Mary as your wife, for the child conceived in her is from the Holy Spirit. She will bear a son, and you are to name him Jesus, for he will save his people from their sins.' All this took place to fulfil what had been spoken by the Lord through the prophet: 'Look, the virgin shall conceive and bear a son, and they shall name him Emmanuel,' which means 'God is with us.' When Joseph awoke from sleep, he did as the angel of the Lord commanded him; he took her as his wife, but had no marital relations with her until she had borne a son; and he named him Jesus.
>
> Matthew 1.18–25

The child is announced with his name, and with that name comes the purpose for which he is born, for which he is to live: to save his people from their sins. Not only is he named, therefore, but so also is the danger in which the people stand and from which they are to be rescued. He fulfils the ancient prophecy of the birth of Emmanuel (Isaiah 7.14) who is the sign of God's intended action, but Jesus' name is specifically the announcement of his mission.

The power of the name which the Jerusalem authorities wanted suppressed when it had been used in the healing of the man at the Beautiful Gate begins to be clearer. The mission and purpose of Jesus are all of one piece from his birth, through his life and death, and on into the activity of the early Church. By the time Peter met the lame man at the Beautiful Gate, 'Yahweh-has-saved' was no mere name or prophecy; it had been lived out in the experience of the people and was being continued in the experience of the early Christian community. It continued to be the means whereby God's power to heal was known, and at the same time to threaten the Jerusalem authorities and demand their action to suppress it. Experiences of rescue, of 'Yahweh-has-saved', were widespread and immensely varied. The name of Jesus was what united those experiences; and in subsequent generations that name would continue to be the instrument of rescue, the continuation of God's power to save the lost, to bring light to those in darkness and at the same time to strike with fear the powers that be.

The name of Jesus captures both the power and the ambiguity, the proclamation and the room for serious misunderstanding, that are major features of his life and work. He is the 'Yahweh-has-saved' for his generation, and then for every generation, destined to rescue his people, to lead them from the wilderness to the land of promise. As such he brings release and healing. On the other hand, he is *Yahweh*-has-saved, reserving to himself the right, as it were, not just to effect the rescue but also, and at the same time, to be their judge: 'You shall call him Jesus, because he will save his people *from their sins.*' In so far as the Gospels describe the unfolding of a tragedy, it is the tragedy of a people who wished to be provided with rescue without accepting God's naming of the peril in which they stood. As an occupied and humiliated power, they knew what would count as rescue for them. Having decided on the rescue they needed, and being convinced that they knew the nature of the peril from which they needed deliverance, they felt sure that this rescuer was not from God, was not the 'Yahweh-has-saved' for whom they were looking, and so they could treat him accordingly. On the other hand, those whose experience of faith led them to accept both the peril as Jesus described it, and the rescue which he offered, knew that he had indeed been appropriately named, given by God 'the name which is above every name, so that at the name of Jesus every knee should bend, in heaven and on earth and under the earth, and every tongue should confess that Jesus Christ is Lord to the glory of God the Father' (Philippians 2.9–11).

'IT IS THE CALLING THAT CREATES THE PERSON'[4]

The power of address to change the person is something which has already been mentioned. Paul Tournier records, among other examples, the experience of encountering in Romania a huge prevalence of Roman names – Trajan, Livia, Virgil – because of the immense pride Romanians take in their Latin roots; thus the naming of children in that way declares that it is their destiny to live up to the best in their national inheritance.

I recall very vividly the day on which my class teacher announced to our class that my surname had changed because of a decision my parents took, and receiving a round of applause (by command of the teacher!) though without any explanation. My parents' decision represented a choice on their part, as people who had come to England during the Nazi years, to integrate fully into their British surroundings, to make their origin a matter which they could reveal or not as they chose, rather than have it revealed automatically every time our family name was used. As I look back, this changed form of address was in effect a command, a statement of how we were to be regarded, a prescription that was decisive for the future. The same is true of the changing of names at adoption: the new name is a sign of the change of family; it is a decision taken for one future rather than another, the new instead of the old.

The language of adoption draws our immediate attention to the way in which believers have from the beginning entered the realm of salvation. From earliest times it has been accompanied by the giving of a name, a practice repeated often at crucial later stages in the life of the believer: at confirmation or ordination or entry into a religious community. But most significantly baptism is itself an entry into the realm of the name of Jesus, the commonwealth in which his authority is recognized. Hence Paul can appeal to the baptismal experience:

> Now I appeal to you, brothers and sisters, by the name of our Lord Jesus Christ, that all of you be in agreement and that there be no division among you, but that you be united in the same mind and the same purpose. For it has been reported to me by Chloe's people that there are quarrels among you, my brothers and sisters. What I mean is that each of you says, 'I belong to Paul' or 'I belong to Apollos' or 'I belong to Cephas' or 'I belong to Christ.' Has Christ been divided? Was Paul crucified for you? Or were you baptized in the name of Paul? I thank God that I baptized none of you except Crispus and Gaius, so that no one can say that you were baptized in my name.
>
> 1 Corinthians 1.10–15

Thus there is no question to whom all of them belong: they were all baptized in(to) the name of the Lord Jesus. They have entered the realm of Jesus, and that realm belongs to 'Yahweh-has-saved'. They are thereby committed both to the diagnosis his name implied, 'for he will save his people from their sins', and to the activity for which he was sent.

THE POWER OF NAMELESSNESS

There is nothing more distressing than facing a peril you

cannot name, and no more powerful a way of keeping people in subjection than hiding from them the sources of power and the names of those responsible for the situation in which they find themselves. This is true no less in the arena of public policy than in that of private distress. To know that something is wrong, but not to know what it is, is to be almost bound to take upon yourself the blame as well as the sensation of distress. To 'get to the bottom of it' means being able to name the issue, not simply in general terms but in a way that carries the conviction that a specific diagnosis of your situation has been reached. Even if the news is bad, it is so much easier to deal with if its nature is not evaded – 'it's a virus'; 'there's a lot of it about' – but given its name. Similarly, much of the power of deep anxiety states and inner distress disappears when, through the processes of analysis or psychotherapy, you have been able to give a specific name to the episode or the experience that lies at the root of your present difficulty.

The power of nameless hurt is amply illustrated by what happened when 'Yahweh-has-saved' came to encounter the possessed man in the country of the Gerasenes:

> When he saw Jesus, he fell down before him and shouted at the top of his voice, 'What have you to do with me, Jesus, Son of the Most High God? I beg you, do not torment me' – for Jesus had commanded the unclean spirit to come out of the man. (For many times it had seized him; he was kept under guard and bound with chains and shackles, but he would break the bonds and be driven by the demon into the wilds.) Jesus then asked him, 'What is your name?' He said, 'Legion'; for many demons had entered him.
>
> Luke 8.28–30[5]

In Mark's account, it is the demons who reply in the plural, calling themselves simply by their huge number; here in St Luke, the person's identity has been completely taken over by his distress, so that the only name available to him is the designation of sources of distress as numerous as the thousands of soldiers in a Roman legion. His distress has no name; but his rescuer has, and restores him to his true identity.

So much of the activity and teaching of Jesus was aimed at pointing his audience in the direction where their peril lay and thereby showing them in what rescue would consist. He names the religious motivation and ambition of his principal critics: they like the best places in the synagogue, they like the popular reverence in which they are held when they make a show of religious observance. The naming of these motivations is the first step to disarming them and saving people from their power.

It is that naming in specific terms that attracts both the following and the opposition: the common people understand the connections he is making and the sense of a new way of relating to God which would not condemn them to the status of outcasts. The religious authorities for their part find themselves named and identified by him. He speaks of them not (except ironically) as the righteous, a name of which they would have been glad, but as the source of the sins of those whom they condemn, and as those who lay burdens on others that they will not carry themselves. Thus they are the apt precursors of those later authorities who forbade the disciples to teach in the name of Jesus and remonstrated with the earliest Christians when they continued to do so.

The role of the naming of perils in rescuing from them can be well illustrated by the use of an entirely secular, contemporary example. The inner city disturbances of 1991 provoked a major public debate about the causes of urban violence and crime. The debate had polarized around the issue of whether unemployment *caused* people to turn to criminal activity. However, in her examination and analysis of these disturbances on Tyneside and elsewhere, the writer Beatrix Campbell gives a very radical account of the present state of British society. Using the perspective provided by those disturbances, Campbell offers a number of clues to understanding them and the society within which they occurred. She *names* some of the key elements in those disturbances, in ways that were certainly unfashionable. She names *masculinity* as one of the major areas of crisis; she *names* the motor car as a key focus of that crisis. She draws a compelling parallel between the status and income which men in some urban communities had been able to derive from their part in the *manufacture* of cars, and the status that could only be derived, now that opportunities for employment in the motor industry had disappeared, by *racing* stolen vehicles around urban housing estates. By the features Campbell *names*, she is able to shed new light on contentious subjects such as car crime and the violence that erupted in the communities she examines.

Furthermore she makes connections between the aggression of the young males at the centre of the riots and the actions of the young men in the police force. That is a connection that is bound to be controversial. At the same time however it does provide an inescapable reminder of the extent to which it has been the women who have hitherto provided much of the social cohesion in many working-class communities. It is their mechanisms of control that are being progressively disempowered as male violence increases and the police retaliate. Her interpretation undermines much of the rhetoric about crime and law and order in ways which neither the political right nor the political left will find palatable, but which we may sense come far closer to the root of the problem than many of the slogans that dominate the debate about crime and the inner city.

Her naming does not end there. She states: 'After a decade of Thatcherism a large cohort of young men and women found themselves not only on the edge of politics, but exiled from the social world. They were neither legitimate citizens nor consumers. Mass unemployment among teenagers, the generation which constitutes the largest "criminal" category, priced them out of social institutions altogether.'[6]

When she details and illustrates her diagnosis of events

Campbell introduces various factors in explanation of what had taken place. When she states that this was happening 'after a decade of Thatcherism' she is *naming* a diagnosis in a way that connects what she is describing with a philosophy and a set of economic policies, personalizing them and relating them to a whole series of developments in society. Many will disagree with her naming of the peril, as many disagreed very deeply also with Margaret Thatcher's own very frequent naming of various 'enemies within'. The point is simply that rescue is not going to be accomplished without naming, the naming of the peril and the naming of the rescue. Generality will not suffice, and the power of Legion will only be brought to heel by the one who is prepared to demand Legion's name and then name what might be the source of rescue for a world in peril.

Campbell also gives a name to her book as its title: *Goliath*. It is a name redolent of primeval male conflict, of victory achieved over what was on the face of it superior force and armour. We are to see in that name a multiplicity of pictures of young people confronting the police and taking over whole areas of territory for themselves. We are to see in it the long history of male aggression, its disastrous effects on the lives of communities and its marginalization of the most vulnerable, mostly women with children. Her book in its very direct naming of the perils and disasters by which 'Britain's Dangerous Places' are nearly overwhelmed makes a much needed contribution to the essential debate about what is to be done at the level of specific, *named* issues and remedies. Readers of the New Testament should not expect rescue to be accomplished without that; rescue begins to come close when causes that are 'Legion' come to be identified.

'YAHWEH-HAS-SAVED'
I have been concerned in this chapter with two distinct but connected points, both of which can be illustrated in relation to the New Testament and to features of our own experience.

First, it has been important to discern what might be meant by speaking of 'Jesus' as the name that saves. His name is specific, and is given for the destiny he is to fulfil. It involved him in both pointing to the peril in which his people stood and becoming in his own person the means by which God will rescue them from it. His name marked out what needed to be done in relation to the society to which he came, and at the same time specified the person who had been marked out to do what needed to be done, naming also his destiny and mission.

My second concern was to draw attention to the important role of naming in the task of rescue. Without our name we cannot be addressed, and that, as Tournier points out, prevents our being individuals and, at the same time, our being 'called', and therefore being members of society. Without naming the diseases which afflict us from time to time we are unable to find any remedy. And the ills of society will remain unresolved until and unless they too are named. In the nature of things that naming will be the subject of some strong disagreement and even violent contention; but the retreat to generality offers no solution, for it leaves our experience as an inchoate mass of different distresses, incapable of being linked to each other. To attempt to name the causes of the social diseases, the injustices and poverty under which people labour, is the absolutely essential first step towards seeking a remedy for them.

If the New Testament offers examples of the power of the saving name, and some of these we have looked at, it also offers some very clear reasons why the naming of our perils is something we shrink from. To name one person, one group, is not to name another; it is to take sides and thereby to generate controversy and the possibility of rejection. It is hardly odd that in the face of the gospel story we prefer teaching that appears general and unlikely to draw excessive attention to the root causes of society's ills. It is not surprising either that in care for individuals and in endeavouring to face our own distresses we are frequently unwilling to come to the specific point, and prefer instead to speak generally. Our strongest reactions, our tears and our anger as much as our delight, are all related to being brought face to face with specific moments, specific responses and specific events. Equally the strongest social disapproval comes to those who see and reveal and who name what they see. They risk the strong reactions that come their way because what they say is inevitably partial and involves the taking of sides. Brueggemann puts this point again in what he says about prophetic theology as opposed to a kind of theology that is content to be general:

> No prophet ever sees things under the aspect of eternity. It is always partisan theology, always for the concrete community, satisfied to see only a piece of it all and to speak out of that at the risk of contradicting the rest of it. Empires prefer systematic theologians who see it all, who understand both sides, and who regard polemics as unworthy of God and divisive of the public good.[7]

In this section, we have paid attention to the saving power of naming names and to the power of the saving name. This in turn takes us on to the content of the life which that name prescribed, to the life that led the earliest Christian disciples to know that 'Yahweh-has-saved' was not merely a name, but a name that was lived, revealed in his words and actions and in the consequent dying that resulted from his naming of names. His was a saving life as well as a saving name, and that was what enabled his followers to declare that this name was above every name, one that elicited the response of worship from all who would hear it.

Where the argument now brings us, therefore, is to the life that brought rescue, to its character as it was observed and described by those who encountered Jesus, and to the nature of the rescue it brought. As with the saving character of the name, however, we shall not enter into that experience unless we bring our life to the reading of the New Testament and allow our life to be the lens through which we look at the saving episodes of Jesus' life. We may expect that if we examine his life in this way we shall be given a greater ability to understand the experience of rescue needed in our time and a greater willingness to receive and share it. As has been our experience in considering the saving name, the New Testament we examine comes in its turn to examine us.

The Life

JESUS RESCUED. TWENTY centuries in which believers have acknowledged him as Saviour have behind them that simple truth. The twenty centuries have in the main focused on his saving death, upon his resurrection and upon the hope of his return to complete the work of salvation and the building of his kingdom. To those matters we shall need to return, for without them the proclamation of Jesus as Saviour makes no sense. But in turn those convictions – of saving death and rising again, and of the completion of his mission to save the world – have their roots in a life that was lived, in rescues that were accomplished, in events that displayed the meaning of his name as the one who, as God's anointed one, brought rescue to those in all kinds of need.

Already in his life, then, Jesus rescued. The power of his name as we discerned it in the previous chapter was known in his life: people were lifted out of potentially disastrous situations, set on their feet, healed, and given a place at tables which, while not the final banquet of heaven, were nevertheless meals that conferred status and meaning. What is more, Jesus spoke a new language, one in which the rhetoric changed from reducing people to enhancing them, from casting them out to including them in. In his life he touched people, not yet with the full power of God's recreative act that would welcome them finally into the kingdom of heaven, but nevertheless with a touch that rescued the unclean from their position as outcasts. In the process much else had to change as well: the rescue was not just of needy individuals, but also of the community of which they were an excluded part.

For that community, the community of God's people, was also to be rescued from the road of exclusion. It had to be rescued from a direction which loaded even greater burdens on those least able to bear them and it had to be turned towards the discovery that the unclean and unwanted were precisely the ones with whom to eat and drink. Jesus rescued, dealing at one and the same time with the pains and griefs of those with whom he came in contact, and with the harsh ways of a society which made their plight worse by interpreting its religious faith in a way that excluded those whom God would most seek to love and to save.

It is this double thrust of Jesus' life of rescue that will concern us in this chapter. It is what has to be grasped if we are to relate to the story of his life as we find it in the Gospels and if we are to connect it with the need for and experience of rescue in our own time. It will also prove essential to an understanding of why his death turned out to be inevitable. His was a double rescue, the saving both of society's victims from their personal distress and of society itself from its continuing capacity to produce victims. That was Jesus' mission, and it brought upon him the judgement of those for whom society's rescue would bring loss of privilege.

THE DOUBLE RESCUE – HEALING AND JUDGEMENT

> It is a gift to meet people associated with the disability rights movement, people who are neither sentimental nor long-suffering about their disabilities. They'll say it stinks – but they're quick to add that the attitude of the culture is far worse than the disability.[1]

Although the New Testament contains much evidence of the persecution to which Christianity was subject, much of it, so far as we can see, was written by people who were, at the time of writing it, not themselves victims. They were reminded that they had 'once been far off, but now were brought near', but the events which the Gospels describe do not themselves appear through the eyes of those who were afflicted. Nevertheless the traces are there; and we can discern them best if we approach the documents through the stories of our contemporaries who speak out of a present experience of being unwelcome and unwanted.

It is not easy to know whether Jesus himself set out with the clarity of purpose that the Church came to read into his every action and word. For all the faith that was read back into the gospel record, there are still traces of events which we may imagine contributed to his own increasing understanding of the way of rescue he was treading. Luke is the evangelist upon whom we have focused most attention so far: he is the one who presents most forcefully the picture of a mission going according to plan, with only the onlookers failing to understand it as it proceeded along its purposeful way. Mark, however, presents an account suggesting that Jesus' double rescue proceeded in a way that was much more out of control. We may recall the comment of one of the bystanders following John F. Kennedy's assassination in Dallas. He described the scene at a dinner where JFK was expected, as the news spread of his shooting: 'For the first time in my life I actually *saw* a rumour.' It is an apt description of the progress of Jesus' ministry as Mark portrays it, a rumour of rescue, not always proceeding under the rescuer's control.

> From there Jesus set out and went away to the region of Tyre. He entered a house and did not want anyone to know he was there. Yet he could not escape notice, but a woman whose little daughter had an unclean spirit immediately heard about him, and she came and bowed down at his feet. Now she was a Gentile, of Syrophoenician origin. She begged him to cast the demon out of her daughter. He said to her, 'Let the children be fed first, for it is not fair to take the children's food and throw it to the dogs.' But she answered him, 'Sir, even the dogs under the table eat the children's crumbs.' Then he said to her, 'For saying that, you may go – the demon has left your daughter.' So she

went home, found the child lying on the bed, and the demon gone.

Mark 7.24–30

This incident has been notoriously difficult for believers, and indeed biblical critics, to handle, for Jesus' answer accords ill with the sentiments we should wish him to express. Much commentary on the passage has all the marks of attempts to justify Jesus to a present-day audience. Perhaps if we had been able to hear his tone of voice we should be clear that he was joking, speculates one; more desperate still is the suggestion that although Jesus' reply seems harsh, the Greek word refers to 'household dogs or puppies', a plea in mitigation that might appeal particularly to the pet-loving English but is unlikely to carry much weight elsewhere, let alone deal with the real difficulty in what Jesus says! It is at least possible that the episode reflects a real moment of truth, a time when the programmatic 'first to the lost sheep of the house of Israel' had to yield to the rumour of rescue spreading with uncontrollable speed and requiring of Jesus a life of response. Certainly the early Church was able to see in such an episode further authority for the mission to the Gentiles.

The rumour of rescue continues in a way that we are told frustrates Jesus' intention to preserve its secrecy. He returns to the Decapolis region, and the rumour again makes its way:

They brought to him a deaf man who had an impediment in his speech; and they begged him to lay his hand on him. He took him aside in private, away from the crowd, and put his fingers into his ears, and he spat and touched his tongue. Then looking up to heaven, he sighed and said to him, 'Ephphatha', that is 'Be opened.' And immediately his ears were opened, his tongue was released, and he spoke plainly. Then Jesus ordered them to tell no one; but the more he ordered them, the more zealously they proclaimed it. They were astounded beyond measure, saying, 'He has done everything well; he even makes the deaf to hear and the mute to speak.'

Mark 7.32–7

This apparently matter-of-fact description of two healings in close succession speaks of the manner of God's rescue at a number of different levels. A girl possessed is rescued from her demon; a man who cannot hear or make himself understood is rescued from his affliction. A Gentile woman is rescued from the place assigned to the dogs and from the position of excluded suppliant to which she, and the countless Gentiles and women of whom she is the precursor and representative, would otherwise have remained consigned.

Even that is not all that these two episodes accomplish. For they also rescue the gospel itself from being confined within what the community of faith might otherwise have sought to control: whatever strategy or narrative construction lay behind the injunctions to secrecy that pepper the Gospel of Mark, it is critical to observe that they did not work, and Mark is entirely clear and candid about that. Unlike Luke's story, Mark's proceeds from an auspicious crowd scene by the Jordan foretelling the imminence of God's reign, via misunderstanding, uncontrollable rumour, malice, insult, abandonment and death to the point where three women by an empty grave receive a message that astonishes them and are too afraid to say anything to anyone. The process that brought healing to the daughter of the Syrophoenician woman and to the man who could not hear or speak is presented as proceeding with a hectic urgency, a process in which Jesus is both agent and respondent. It is a process that comes to make sense only if it is regarded as God's mission and God's rescue.

Not surprisingly, what comes next after the two healings is the gathering of a crowd too large to feed. There follows an altercation with the Pharisees and a conversation with the disciples which they are at a loss to understand, culminating in the rebuke,

'Why are you talking about having no bread? Do you still not perceive or understand? Are your hearts hardened? Do you have eyes, and fail to see? Do you have ears, and fail to hear? And do you not remember? When I broke the five loaves for the five thousand, how many baskets full of broken pieces did you collect?' They said to him, 'Twelve.' 'And the seven for the four thousand, how many baskets full of broken pieces did you collect?' And they said to him, 'Seven.' And he said to them, 'Do you not yet understand?'

Mark 8.17–21

The narrative races on, and the rumour of rescue spreads, unable to be contained. Jesus is the one who seeks to make himself, and the purpose of God, clear; but with each step along the road more revelation produces more misunderstanding, and more compassion engenders more hostility.

The rescue God accomplishes in Jesus cannot be reduced to an operation at one level, a work essentially able to be completed according to plan. Naturally there were those from the very beginning who would have had every reason to seek to present it entirely as a successfully planned enterprise: forget the difficult issues, just keep producing more bread. Stop requiring faith; just produce another sign, and nothing will succeed like success. It is possible to present salvation like that, and often that is how it has been presented.

However, the New Testament, and Mark's Gospel not least, shows clear signs that it was not remembered as having been that way; always there is the New Testament's record of Jesus, and with it the clear evidence that when 'Yahweh saves', there comes about something that is unexpected, the difficult issue to be faced, the question for the community to struggle with. The rescue Jesus offers does lift victims out of their predicament, but always requires at one and the same time not just the feeding of the hungry and the healing of the sick, but also the opening of the ears of an unhearing society so that the mouths of the voiceless can be unstopped.

Painted into the pavement, the familiar logo
Of a blue-and-white wheelchair protects
Ease of access to the library for the disabled:
Their own diagonal parking-stall nearest
Self-opening doors. Protected against disabling
Cars by the library's steel bookdrop, a stub
Of tree of heaven recurs here year after year,
Where the self-opening force of a seed
Fractured the cement like sod. Never to be
A dancing girl of a tree like the new maple
Plantings in the library lawn, flirting a swirl
Of bright leaves, never to grow tall, upright,
Straight-limbed, in winter it drowns in snow
Banked by the bookdrop, in summer thirsts
Through baked concrete, thrusting a stunted
Diagonal that survives, sundances, flaunts
Green, transcends its merely being trapped
In a space reserved for the handicapped.[2]

Jesus rescues hungry people, poor people, blind people, deaf people, lame people; but raising always the question: *who* is hungry, poor, blind, deaf, lame? So there is no escape from the irony as well as the truth of his declaration that 'those who are well have no need of a physician, but those who are sick; I have come to call not the righteous but sinners' (Mark 2.17, Matthew 9.12, Luke 5.31). What Jesus lives out is his name: his eating and drinking with outcasts is for the purpose of witnessing to the way in which 'Yahweh saves', not by separation but by inclusion. What that involves is a twofold direction of salvation, on the one hand towards those in need, and on the other towards a society that perpetuates their exclusion; the rescue of that society requires its conversion, a rescue from itself. To those whose governing text was 'You shall be holy, for I the Lord your God am holy' (Leviticus 19.2), and who interpreted it as meaning 'You shall be separate, for I the Lord your God am separate', Jesus substitutes the governing command, 'Be merciful, just as your Father is merciful' (Luke 6.36); in him holiness and mercy are joined together.[3]

TRUTH TO POWER

The rescue Jesus is about is God's rescue. It involves healing and release to those in greatest need, and at the same time a change of attitude and behaviour in the society at large. Without that, the lot of the helpless is simply made worse. Hence, whatever is the source of their suffering, it cannot be alleviated without that other rescue, the rescue which consists in convicting the community of its tendency to exclude and demean. That in turn requires the speaking of truth to power.

> Then they sent to him some Pharisees and some Herodians to trap him in what he said. And they came and said to him, 'Teacher, we know that you are sincere, and show deference to no one; for you do not regard people with partiality, but teach the way of God in accordance with truth. Is it lawful to pay taxes to the emperor, or not? Should we pay them, or should we not?' But knowing their hypocrisy, he said to them, 'Why are you putting me to the test? Bring me a denarius and let me see it.' And they brought one. Then he said to them, 'Whose head is this, and whose title?' They answered, 'The emperor's'. Jesus said to them, 'Give [back] to the emperor the things that are the emperor's, and [give back] to God the things that are God's.' And they were utterly amazed at him.
>
> Mark 12.13–17

For his interrogators, the power from which the people need to be rescued is the power of the emperor. The trap contained in their question is the obvious one: say yes, and you will lose credibility with the people; say no, and you stand to be reported to the Roman authorities on a charge of subversion. In fact, as it turned out, the nature of his reply made little difference: according to Luke's account, Jesus was in any case accused of 'perverting our nation, forbidding us to pay taxes to the emperor, and saying that he himself is the Messiah, a king' (Luke 23.2).

More significant than the trap, however, is the character of Jesus' response. With the tribute coin held before his hearers, he says first that they must repay (*apodote*) to Caesar what belongs to him. The change of word makes an unmistakable point: Jesus is asked whether tribute should be *given* to Caesar, and replies that it must be *repaid*. The fact is that his interrogators are in debt to the emperor whose coinage they hold; his power and wealth is the source of theirs and they are content to benefit from it when it suits them.[4]

The climax of Jesus' riposte comes, however, with the final words, '. . . and [repay to] God the things that are God's'. Here we have the classic prophetic statement of the point that those in authority have effectively stolen God's people from God, behaving as owners rather than stewards, and treating God's people as though they were their own. Jesus' statement is a recall to the truth that the people is God's and not the property of those in power; the demand of God is for faithfulness to God's call, and those in authority have no right to come between God and God's own. God's rescue of the people will consist not in the removal of the emperor's jurisdiction but in restitution to those in need and repentance by those in power.

This altercation displays quite clearly what is then the unmistakable meaning of the parable of the debtors in Matthew 18: a king wishes to settle account with his slaves, and in the process forgives an enormous debt to one of them who is unable to pay. That same slave refuses to remit a much smaller debt owed him by one of his fellow-slaves; as a result the king is furious.

'Then his lord summoned him and said to him, "You wicked slave! I forgave you all that debt because you pleaded with me. Should you not have had mercy on your fellow slave, as I had mercy on you?" And in anger his lord handed him over to be tortured until he would pay his entire debt. So my heavenly Father will also do to every one of you, if you do not forgive your brother or sister from your heart.'

The parable is placed as a response to Peter's question about the number of times he should forgive someone who sins against him, and in illustration of Jesus' response, 'not till seven times but seventy times seven'. Yet it is also making a more widely subversive statement too: by the end of the parable the king is a 'lord' (*kyrios*) and a contrast is being drawn between the massive indebtedness of the punitive slave and the minor debt of his fellow-slave. That makes a significant comment yet again on who is righteous and who is the sinner in the community of God's people. The point is clearly made: an enormous restitution is required by those who rule or bear authority; and yet their response is not repentance, but the imposition of unbearable burdens on those whose need to make restitution is vastly smaller.

The rescue of God is always first and foremost a reassertion of God's authority over individuals and communities; and that has to mean that the message of rescue has to be understood and received with repentance by those who wield power. The message is clearly spelled out in the way in which Jesus in John 10 appropriates the image of shepherding, with its long history of use in connection with the direction of God's people by its earthly rulers. When Jesus speaks of himself as the 'good shepherd' who 'lays down his life for the sheep' he does so in clear contrast with those other 'shepherds of Israel' who are to be described as thieves and bandits, hirelings and strangers, unlike the true shepherd who knows his own and leads them out to pasture.

The language is of rescue from false shepherding by the true shepherd, the one who fulfils the prophecy Ezekiel addressed to the 'shepherds of Israel', a prophecy which is also highly critical of those who exercise power in their own interests:

> Thus says the Lord God: Ah, you shepherds of Israel who have been feeding yourselves! Should not shepherds feed the sheep? You eat the fat, you clothe yourselves with the wool, you slaughter the fatlings, but you do not feed the sheep. You have not strengthened the weak, you have not healed the sick, you have not bound up the injured, you have not brought back the strayed, you have not sought the lost, but with force and harshness you have ruled them. So they were scattered because there was no shepherd; and scattered, they became food for all the wild animals. My sheep were scattered, they wandered over all the mountains and on every high hill; my sheep were scattered over all the face of the earth, with no one to search or seek for them.
>
> Ezekiel 34.2–6

Because of their self-serving failure to act as shepherds, God declares Godself against the shepherds, and then promises to act in the only way possible to rescue the situation:

> I myself will search for my sheep, and will seek them out. As shepherds seek out their flocks when they are among their scattered sheep, so I will seek out my sheep. I will rescue them from all the places in which they have been scattered on a day of clouds and thick darkness ... I myself will be the shepherd of my sheep, and I will make them lie down, says the Lord God. I will seek the lost, and I will bring back the strayed, and I will bind up the injured, and I will strengthen the weak, but the fat and the strong I will destroy. I will feed my sheep with justice.
>
> Ezekiel 34.11–12, 15–16

The account of Jesus' shepherding carries forward into his day, and then into the life of the kingdom of God, all the judgement and threat of the words of the prophet to those who wield power if they forget whose servants they are and in whose interests they are always to act. The parable of the judgement ('the sheep and the goats') in Matthew 25 expresses the divine concern for the 'least of the brothers and sisters'. How else could it end, in the light of the words of Ezekiel which must have inspired it?

> As for you, my flock, thus says the Lord God: I shall judge between sheep and sheep, between rams and goats. Is it not enough for you to feed on the good pasture, but you must tread down with your feet the rest of your pasture? When you drink of clear water, must you foul the rest with your feet? And must my sheep eat what you have trodden with your feet, and drink what you have fouled with your feet?
>
> Ezekiel 34.17–19

In carrying out God's rescue, Jesus acts for God and claims to be doing so by the language he uses of himself. Integral to the rescue he is carrying out is a word to those exercising power, and the word is that they have abused their prerogative and accordingly will lose it. The rescue of God brings release to those in need; at the same time it addresses the society as a whole; and above all it is truth addressed to power.

Nobody considering this feature of God's rescue as the New Testament describes it can avoid having in mind all that our own century has brought to pass. It has seen enough enduring tyrannies to leave anyone reading the Scriptures with the searing question, how could they endure so long and perpetrate such cruelty? In the face of the terrible excesses of totalitarianism that have been witnessed in our time, is it still possible to base our hope on what the New Testament has to say about the relationship of power to justice? Many have had good cause to doubt the Bible's promise that God is indeed determined to rescue the needy. Can such claims, about the conditional nature of all human authority and the threat which that implies to those who wield power unjustly, be anything more than empty words to those who remember the Holocaust or the Gulag? And current examples of dictatorship and genocide may be numerically smaller than their predecessors, but they raise just the same question.

Yet at the same time believers in a divine rescue that includes a divine judgement upon abuses of power have in this same century seen developments that bring confirmation to their faith as well as fulfilment to their hopes. Events as far apart as the bringing down of the Berlin wall or the victories won against racism in the United States and South Africa, seen from the perspective of the New Testament, witness to that judgement; they declare that the life of Christ is to be seen in the subversion of unjust rule, and they remind believers that those who preach the gospel of rescue have both the freedom and the charge to continue to speak truth to power. They are still to call for the restoration to God of the things of God, and to expect that the relief of those in need will involve hard repentance for those who, while they occupy the place of the shepherd in their society, behave more like the hireling or the robber.

TO HEAL OUR YESTERDAY

It is hard to exaggerate the power of past injury, and there are few things human beings need more than to be able to deal with the hurts they have received in their past and then move on. High among the lessons of this century has been what we have come to know about the power of past damage in people's lives.

We have seen that truth working itself out politically. What conflict activates in relations between nations is the long catalogue of bad memories that retain an enormous hold on peoples, and no peace can be secured in such situations without disarming those memories. What caused pain in the past has not to be forgotten; rather it has to be remembered in a way that does not keep conflict alive. It is not the memories themselves that do the damage but the way in which they can be pressed into the service of current arguments, continuing to arouse passions and thereby to prevent problems and possibilities from being looked at with any kind of freshness. The legacy of the past is often literally paralysing, something from which we urgently need rescue if our current needs are to be addressed.

Then some people came, bringing to him a paralysed man, carried by four of them. And when they could not bring him to Jesus because of the crowd, they removed the roof above him; and after having dug through it, they let down the mat on which the paralytic lay. When Jesus saw their faith, he said to the paralytic, 'Son your sins are forgiven.' Now some of the scribes were sitting there, questioning in their hearts, 'Why does this fellow speak in this way? It is blasphemy! Who can forgive sins but God alone?' At once Jesus perceived in his spirit that they were discussing these questions among themselves, and he said to them, 'Why do you raise such questions in your hearts? Which is easier, to say to the paralytic, "Your sins are forgiven," or to say, "Stand up and take your mat and walk"? But so that you may know that the Son of Man has authority on earth to forgive sins' – he said to the paralytic – 'I say to you, stand up, take your mat and go to your home.' And he stood up, and immediately took the mat and went out before all of them; so that they were all amazed and glorified God, saying, 'We have never seen anything like this.'

Mark 2.3–12

Mark places this story very close to the beginning of Jesus' ministry. It is only the second specific account of a healing, and begins the series that appears in Mark 2.1—3.6 of conflicts which Jesus has with the religious leaders. The Marcan pace is already rapid; the rumour of rescue is spreading fast, for already the leper Jesus has healed (1.40–5)

53

has broadcast the fact, with the result that Jesus 'could not go into a town openly'. What is described as the 'faith' of the paralysed man's friends includes their desperate urgency in approaching Jesus; but Jesus' response does not on the face of it appear to address the urgency of the man's present need at all. 'Your sins are forgiven', he declares, evidently going to the root of what appeared on the surface as simply a physical disability.

The result is dramatic. The conflict that ensues might appear to us to be an entirely abstract one, and not concerned with the needs of the paralytic at all, a conflict over whether any human being, and that specifically means Jesus, has authority to forgive. Yet in another way it is a conflict about the critical significance of the rescue Jesus offers. The power of the paralytic's sins is overcome, and with it the capacity of his sins to decide his status in the present. God's forgiveness of the paralysed man does not merely affect his particular condition. It also asserts Jesus' power as God's agent to free persons from the effects of the discrimination which they suffered as 'sinners'. Thus Jesus' action also brings to an end the paralytic's status as 'sinner' and therefore his marginal status in the society of which he was a part. It is not at all surprising that the guardians of society's moral hierarchy, those with jurisdiction over who was to be classed as sinner and who not, took issue with Jesus' action; here was an act of rescue that did not simply meet an individual's need, but at the same time spoke a word of truth that threatened the exercise of religious power.

Here, however, we need to notice another aspect of the story. The religious leaders do not take responsibility for their particular role in the exclusion which the paralysed man as sinner experiences. That responsibility, they are clear, rests with God, 'who alone can forgive sins'. Human beings can only be released from the entail of their sin by God – and so long as that is true it means in effect that we are helpless to unlock the personal and social paralysis created by the hurts of anybody's past. Jesus however acts for God, revealing that God's desire is different, not exclusion but inclusion, not a locking into hurt but a releasing from it. In taking upon himself the divine prerogative of forgiveness, Jesus makes totally clear the connection between the paralysis of the man's limbs and the paralysis imposed by a social structure which effectively prevents his being fully a part of the community. His is a power that is determined to transcend anyone's 'being trapped in a space reserved for the handicapped'.

According to Mark and Luke, the bystanders are amazed, in Luke's case mystified by 'the strange things we have seen today'. From Matthew, however, we hear that they were afraid at what they had seen. They had reason to be, for this event contained the message of a profound change, one in which the security of an accustomed social order was about to be overturned. They gave glory to God 'who had given such authority to human beings' (Matthew 9.8). Jesus acts for God, doing what it was believed only God could do in relation to people's sins; in the process he witnesses to something which concerns not just his status and authority, but that of all human persons. The unlocking of the injuries of the past is a crucial part of God's purpose, and at the same time one entrusted to human beings. They can no longer disclaim the responsibility they have for whether they release people from the entail of past hurt and transgression or choose instead to imprison them in it. Here we have a real foreshadowing of what the risen Christ in the Fourth Gospel offers to the community of believers:

> When it was evening on that day, the first day of the week, and the doors of the house where the disciples had met were locked for fear of the Jews, Jesus came and stood among them and said, 'Peace be with you.' After he said this he showed them his hands and his side. Then the disciples rejoiced when they saw the Lord. Jesus said to them again, 'Peace be with you. As the Father has sent me,

so I send you.' When he had said this, he breathed on them and said to them, 'Receive the Holy Spirit. If you forgive the sins of any they are forgiven them; if you retain the sins of any they are retained.'

John 20.19–23

Christ, who has rescued human beings from being trapped in an understanding of religious belief that excludes 'sinners' from the life of the community, now creates a community of faith which has authority to continue his ministry of release and of judgement. Thus the life of Jesus, and the authority given to him by God, is handed on to the community of his followers; they too are to continue the rescue of God's people from their sins, and at the same time to take issue with all that continues to imprison people.

A similar releasing of a person, involving also a taking issue with social attitudes that imprison her, occurs in the quite different context of Jesus' encounter with the Samaritan woman at the well in John 4.[5] Her conversation with him is robust and engaging, and among the most significant aspects of it is the variety of ways in which the encounter exhibits a freedom from the constraints imposed by social conventions. She is described at the outset not by name but simply as 'a Samaritan woman'; the phrase signifies that she is there as representative as well as individual, and at the same time it alerts us at once to the possibility that constraining social boundaries are about to be broken. Sure enough, both as Samaritan and as woman she is the occasion of something new. The traditional conflict between Jew and Samaritan about where God is to be worshipped is transcended:

The woman said to him, 'Sir I see you are a prophet. Our ancestors worshipped on this mountain, but you say that the place where people must worship is in Jerusalem.' Jesus said to her, 'Woman, believe me, the hour is coming when you will worship the Father neither on this mountain nor in Jerusalem. You worship what you do not know; we worship what we know, for salvation comes from the Jews. But the hour is coming, and is now here, when the true worshippers will worship God in spirit and truth.

John 4.19–24

Similarly, we read of the disciples' astonishment that Jesus is found speaking with a woman, 'but no one said "What do you want?" or "Why are you speaking with her?"'. We see here a double freedom to open doors that convention would have kept closed, and the implication of this is of a rescue that can include the whole world: 'And many more believed because of his word. They said to the woman, "It is no longer because of what you said that we believe, for we have heard for ourselves, and we know that this is truly the Saviour of the world"' (John 4.41, 42).

The relationship of Jesus to the structure of the society in which he lived, and the way in which God deprives it of its power, are crucial here. We receive the impression often that forgiveness is a divine act of forgetting, and this is supported by a number of texts which suggest exactly that: 'I will forgive their iniquity, and remember their sin no more.' But this is not in our sense a 'forgetting' of past hurt, as though it had never been; rather it is a divine resolve not to act as though it were decisive for the present. The injuries of the past are deprived of their power to imprison; but this is not by pretending that what has happened has not happened. It is by acting in freedom, not allowing what has been to be determinative of what is to be in the future. Through God's transformation, entrusted to Jesus in his lifetime and committed then to the community of faith, past harm is not simply wiped out: it becomes *felix culpa*, fault that is a source of blessing, the raw material of a far better future.

The distinction is vital: what happens to the constraints people suffer, be it the sins they have committed, the illnesses with which they are afflicted, or the inferior status to which they have been confined, is that they are enabled not to be decisive. Rather they form part of the process of rescue by which others in their turn can be released. The nationality, status and past experience of believers are not forgotten; they retain what they bring into the life of the believing community, but as gift and not as condemnation. Thus Paul is able to refer to people's nationality, educational level, and relationship to God's covenant with Israel, and frequently does so.

> Consider your own call, brothers and sisters; not many of you were wise by human standards, not many were powerful, not many were of noble birth. But God chose what is foolish in the world to shame the wise; God chose what is weak in the world to shame the strong; God chose what is low and despised in the world, things that are not, to reduce to nothing things that are, so no one might boast in the presence of God.
>
> 1 Corinthians 1.26–9

Jesus saw in the paralytic lying on his mat evidence of a need for rescue, not just of him but of a whole people who treated such a man as a sinner, held down by a burden from which no human being could release him. Paul make clear that 'boasting' is just as much a sign of the need for rescue; for both the boasting of those with status and the burdens of those without are signs of constraining conventions that include some and exclude others. The rescue of God lifts unsustainable burdens, at the same time as it threatens the powerful and strong.

The parallels from all kinds of situations today are very evident. Those who find themselves in personal difficulties frequently take those difficulties to a person whose skills lie precisely in enabling people to return to parts of their past that continue to have destructive power over them in the present. Many of the psychotherapeutic disciplines which have blossomed in this century are based on an approach to the past which is grounded not in our capacity to forget, but on the contrary our *in*capacity to forget the past. The processes of therapy assume that almost every episode from our past life, and most of all those which have exercised some emotional power over us, is imprinted on our memory; our problem is that we *cannot* forget. What has to be done is to return the past to our conscious mind, to address the source of its power, and thereby to make it into something which, having previously controlled our lives without our recognizing it, can now be a resource to be used in our self-understanding, and therefore in our capacity to be of sensitive help to others.

Such an approach to the past is not however only to be found in our dealing with the personal difficulties of individuals.[6] What is true of individuals has also to be true of communities and nations. The desperate conflicts of Ireland and the Sudan and the wounds scored into the memories of the inhabitants of Bosnia or the Middle East cannot ever possibly be forgotten. The children of civil war, of refugee camps or of the 'peace line' bear a burden which cannot possibly be erased from their minds. What has to be longed for – and it is a miracle even greater than forgetting – is that the stories of former enemies might come to be shared, might become part of a new, common, story.

We have witnessed in recent times the overcoming of some particularly oppressive patterns of injustice, all of which have raised the question, how the pain of a divided past is to be understood and dealt with. For when injustice is overcome, it always raises the question how the period of the previous oppression is to be handled, and what are to be the mechanisms of forgiveness. This issue has been particularly poignant recently as people have watched in amazement the radical change that has taken place in South Africa, and wondered in fear and trembling whether some form of retribution would be exacted from those who previously had acted as oppressors. Yet we hear even now the first beginnings of that sharing of experiences of Afrikaners and Black people there, of the comparable injuries sustained by both communities in their past, which could be the raw materials of a new shared history stretching into the future. That is a vastly more creative hope than the vain expectation that the terrible years of apartheid might be forgotten.

To the extent that such a future is beginning to emerge, it shows that those who have now assumed the responsibility of power have committed themselves to what is certain to be an immensely difficult task: to retain their clarity about what the issue at stake in their struggle was, that it was not about the victory of one culture that had been downtrodden over another that had held the reins of power. That is to say, the memory is not of a struggle to gain the upper hand for a set of ethnic and cultural traditions, previously enslaved; rather it was to cause a diversity of culture and history to be deprived of its power to produce conflict and oppression and made, instead, into a shared experience and resource for the inclusion of all the people into a common future.

Do we not see here some image of the character of Christ's rescue of people from debilitating social structures, and of his determination to interrupt the process by which hurts carried as a burden down the years come to be used to control the lives of people in the present? He comes to his society and its neediest members; he confronts and names destructive attitudes which continue to be decisive in terms of people's present and future lives; and by so doing he allows them to bring their life and their experience as a resource for the common life of the community of faith.

The rescue of God has to do with that kind of reshaping of past injury. Jesus dealt in his life with those for whom the pattern of their society was enslaving and disabling. In the process he called into being a community committed to a new way of using and sharing the various gifts and experiences which its members brought to the common life. That meant challenging attitudes and conventions that had become instruments of exclusion, and proclaiming and offering a pattern of release.

It also meant something else: the posing of a strong challenge to those who had moulded their community in their own image, who had used it for their own interests, and who were determined to find divine authority for their status in society and the privilege which they enjoyed. That meant, once again, the confrontation involved in speaking truth to power, in the service of rescuing the people from the exclusion which they suffered:

Then Pharisees and scribes came to Jesus from Jerusalem and said, 'Why do your disciples break the traditions of the elders? For they do not wash their hands before they eat.' He answered them, 'And why do you break the commandment of God for the sake of your tradition? For God said, "Honour your father and your mother," and, "Whoever speaks evil of father or mother must surely die." But you say that whoever tells father or mother, "Whatever support you might have had from me is given to God", then that person need not honour the father. So for the sake of your tradition, you make void the word of God. You hypocrites! Isaiah prophesied rightly about you when he said "This people honours me with their lips, but their hearts are far from me; in vain do they worship me, teaching human precepts as doctrines."'

Matthew 15.1–9

The world confronts us, as it did Jesus and his followers, with a huge range of burdens from which release is required. It also, as we have seen, demonstrates from time to time the first signs of a harvest of rescue in progress. What the Gospels present is an engagement with those burdens and a commitment to that harvest which go to the deepest levels of human need. They touch not merely the burden of sickness, but also the weight of guilt; they release people not just from the pain they know about or choose to present, but also from the weight of memory and history which has not yet come to the surface of their consciousness or which they would rather conceal from themselves. As well as that kind of depth, however, the rescue God brought in Jesus engages with what religious faith has found it less easy to accommodate, the connection between the ills of the most vulnerable and the abuses of power and trust that determine the shape of society as a whole.

The way of rescue, therefore, had to involve confrontation with the holders of power in the society, for its traditions, including its most solemn religious traditions, had become a tool in their hands, used against God's purpose. We have seen in this chapter that there was no possibility of rescuing society's victims from their distress without a deliberate facing up to the ways in which society's structures and those who administered them in some cases actually created those victims and in nearly every case added to their hurt. Jesus' life, as we have seen, was given to that rescue, and in the process to that confrontation. And it is there that we find the clue to what has been acknowledged down the generations as his final and decisive act of rescue, namely his death. And it is to the paradox of how a death might save that we now turn.

4

The Death

DEATH IS NO RESCUE

'Let us demonstrate by our presence at this great event that although they have destroyed our industry they cannot destroy our traditions.'

from a leaflet advertising the Durham Miners' Gala of 1994

As I write this the city of Durham is echoing to the sound of brass bands, pipes and drums, and is resplendent with the banners of miners' lodges and regional trade union and Labour party branches. It is the day of the 110th Durham Miners' Gala. The traditions are indeed long-standing and impressive. The Durham Big Meeting was attended at its height by crowds running into six figures, and no leading Labour politicians would decline the honour of being there, or the opportunity of making a major statement of policy to rouse the warriors in the struggle, and in the process enhance their own credibility as leaders.

Yet nobody can be unaware that though this may be the 110th in a distinguished line of such events, it is also in another and much more depressing sense a new situation. It is the first time that such a gala has taken place when there is not a single pit left open in the Durham coalfield. That was the coalfield where once one quarter of all miners in Britain had worked, and that at a time when one quarter of all trade unionists in Britain were miners and ten per cent of all children in this country were brought up in a miner's household.[1] That means that this gala is also an occasion surrounded by great sadness.

That is not of course to demean the organization of this particular day, or its contribution to maintaining the pride and dignity of those who take part in it. In a manner reminiscent of the way in which the miners returned to their pits behind their banners and their bands after the defeated strike of 1984, this gala represents a refusal to 'go gentle into that good night' that deserves every respect. The acknowledgement of their history and the observance of their traditions preserve at least an inner dignity. They refuse to allow those who have destroyed their livelihood, their communities and their way of life, to take away their pride and their memories as well. In holding on to the tradition of the gala, they also hold on to the vision and the values that the past represented. So without doubt it is better that there should have been today rather than not.

But there is no rescue, no hope of restoration. Except on a very small scale, there is no chance of the industry being revived, and if and when it is, it will not, as it once did, shape the way of life of whole communities and counties. For many of the individuals involved there is not even much sign of rescue in the form of a new job. There may be those who thought little of that former way of life, and certainly much of its working practice was hard and dangerous; certainly many did not want their sons to repeat their working experience. In that sense there may be relief for some, but of rescue not a sign. There is no rescue in death, not even in the death of an industry.

I have started here, with a tiny summary of a piece of social experience, because the death of Jesus was also and among many other things likewise a piece of social experience. It was also, and not in the least in any metaphorical sense, a death, the death of a particular person at a particular time and place – under Pontius Pilate, outside Jerusalem. But in our attempt to approach the New Testament on the basis of the links which it makes with our own experience, we need to be clear that Jesus' death was the death of more than Jesus, and to that we shall return in a moment.

First, though, it is important to say that, even had we started from our direct experience of the deaths of individuals, we should still have had to make a similar point: death is no rescue. We may sometimes say, after the death of someone elderly or racked with the discomfort of a serious illness, that death came as a release; but even then that sense is often clouded with our unresolved distress over the suffering from which death released the dying person. If they had to die, we may feel, it is a relief that death came quickly; but the 'if they had to die' speaks of our sense that the loss which is death is a reality which cannot be gainsaid or mitigated. We have said and believed for so long that the death of Jesus brought salvation to the world that we have to be reminded firmly that there is nothing intrinsically saving about death; there is no rescue in it. Only if we are clear about that can we begin to discern what Christians might mean when they say of this particular death that it was the means of salvation for the world; we need to be aware that in making that proclamation we are saying something altogether novel and remarkable.

This is particularly important for an understanding of the New Testament witness on this subject; for despite the fact that its writers wrote from a position of faith and from the experience of the Christian community, they do not seek to conceal the overwhelming sense of loss involved in Jesus' death, and certainly if they did seek to conceal that loss they did not succeed. For the sense of radical disappointment, and of the enormity of what is involved in continuing to speak of Jesus' death as saving despite that loss, is evident in at least three aspects: the sense of the strong desire of Jesus, as his disciples remembered him, to avoid death if that could be; the horror with which the disciples greeted the prediction, and then the fact, of Jesus' death; and their sense that to speak of that death to others as saving would arouse only incredulity and rejection.

JESUS AND HIS OWN DYING
Much can be made of the impossibility of knowing when, to what extent, and with what inner feelings, Jesus in fact

approached the prospect of meeting his death at the hands of those whom his teaching, miracles and announcement of the kingdom of God offended. It is true that we have no autobiographical record of his feelings on this (or any other) matter, and many of the moments when we are offered what appear to be insights into his state of mind, such as the so-called agony in the Garden of Gethsemane, must have been reconstructions rather than recollections, for there is no record that anyone was in a position to observe them.

Nevertheless, there are some clear common threads in the way the story of Jesus' approach to his death is told, despite very large differences in the accounts we have. Put simply they come down to two central points: Jesus did predict his own suffering and death, and shared this prediction with his disciples; and the thought of that suffering and death troubled him deeply.

Mark's framework locates the first foretelling immediately after the confession of faith in Jesus as Messiah at Caesarea Philippi:

> Then he began to teach them that the Son of Man must undergo great suffering, and be rejected by the elders, the chief priests, and the scribes, and be killed, and after three days rise again. He said all this quite openly. And Peter took him aside and began to rebuke him. But turning and looking at his disciples, he rebuked Peter and said, 'Get behind me, Satan! For you are setting your mind not on divine things but on human things.'
>
> Mark 8.31–3

Matthew (16.21–3) includes a reference to Jesus' foretelling his visit to Jerusalem, and Luke (9.22) omits the reference to Peter's rebuke. The prediction is followed by a statement of the cost of discipleship, and is repeated further on, after the transfiguration. Mark (9.30–2) and Luke (9.43–5) record that the disciples did not understand the saying and were afraid to ask, Matthew (17.22–3) that they were very distressed.

There are other predictions of a less specific sort, about a calamity in which Jesus will be involved. There is the use of the image of baptism, one which had come to carry the note of being overwhelmed,[2] and which the early Christian community had certainly come to understand as referring to Jesus' suffering and death. 'I have come to bring fire to the earth, and how I wish it were already kindled! I have a baptism with which to be baptized, and what stress I am under until it is completed' (Luke 12.49, 50). Given that Jesus' death on the cross is depicted as far more serene than the picture presented in Mark and Matthew, it is particularly significant that Luke does not in any way conceal the sense of foreboding and agony that preceded it. It is with the same sense that Jesus is remembered as saying to James and John, following their request for places of precedence in his kingdom, 'You do not know what you are asking. Are you able to drink the cup that I drink or be baptized with the baptism that I am baptized with?' (Mark 10.36).

John also has Jesus going knowingly to his death: he is presented as predicting Judas' treachery (6.70); in chapter 12 he charges Mary at Bethany to keep the precious ointment for the day of his burial, and further on in the same chapter utters intimations of his death which include some which bear strong impressions of the Gethsemane scene in the other Gospels:

> The hour has come for the Son of Man to be glorified. Very truly, I tell you, unless a grain of wheat falls into the earth and dies, it remains just a single grain; but if it dies, it bears much fruit. Those who love their life lose it, and those who hate their life in this world will keep it for eternal life . . . Now my soul is troubled. And what should I say – 'Father, save me from this hour'? No, it is for this reason that I have come to this hour.
>
> John 12.23–5, 27

The Gethsemane scene itself is the clearest statement that

Jesus is remembered as approaching his death as a struggle in which, despite his foreboding, he submits himself to God's will: one reading of Luke portrays his sweat falling as drops of blood on the ground.

Whatever, then, may have been the precise occasions and manner of any predictions Jesus made about his fate, and whatever anticipation or fear he may in fact have expressed about it, there is no doubt that the gospel records would have us see his suffering and death as foreseen, and as being a source of distress to those who contemplated them; all the evangelists present a portrayal of Jesus which is without doubt that of a person with foreknowledge of his death, and longing for that destiny to be removed from him.

There are, of course, other notes struck as well elsewhere in the New Testament: Jesus is the one to whom Christians look as 'pioneer and perfecter of our faith, who for the sake of the joy that was set before him endured the cross, disregarding its shame, and [so] has taken his seat at the right hand of the throne of God' (Hebrews 12.2). But the sense of resolute obedience is not allowed to conceal that other sense of a death foreseen, and foreseen with great distress. Whatever is the source of the rescue which Jesus' death is believed to have accomplished, those who remembered it and proclaimed the gospel of release through the death of Christ do not seem to be telling us that in and of itself it was an obviously saving event. In death in and of itself, even in the death of Jesus, there is no clear sign of rescue accomplished.

Even if we seek in the passion stories themselves for people who might have been rescued by it, who might have come to represent the saved community of the future early Church, all the signs we are given have to be balanced against the equally evident signs that Jesus' dying was seen as a source of disaster. Although Jesus' condemnation results, according to all four evangelists, from the crowd's demand for the release of Barabbas, and might be said, therefore, to have rescued Barabbas from his fate, this receives no attention at all in the

New Testament.[3] In any case, if we were balancing rescue against disaster, we should have to balance the saving of Barabbas with the suicide of Judas.

Similarly, we should have to balance the 'saving' of the penitent thief, as Luke records it, with the fact that his companion appears not to have found any rescue from either death or bitterness. The centurion at the cross is recorded in the various accounts as making a positive response to the sight of the manner of Jesus' dying, but the passers-by, the soldiers and the religious leaders simply mock at the sight. If they use words that later on come to represent the saving significance of what took place, they do so without knowing their meaning:

> Those who passed by derided him, shaking their heads and saying, 'Aha! You who would destroy the temple in three days, save yourself, and come down from the cross.' In the same way the chief priests, along with the scribes, were also mocking him among themselves and saying, 'He saved others; he cannot save himself. Let the Messiah, the King of Israel, come down from the cross now, so that we may see and believe.'
>
> Mark 15.29–32

The record seems clear: this death was not in any transparent way a rescue. Without the anticipation of it, the sense of its having been foretold by the prophets, and accepted in obedience to the Father's will, this death would have carried no meaning and borne no fruit. Worse: unlike many natural, and even many tragic, deaths, this death would simply have added to the burden of despair carried by those who were looking for liberation and not finding it. Those who came after, if they had heard anything of this story at all, would have found themselves aptly represented by Cleopas. When he discusses these events with a stranger on the way to Emmaus, he expresses more than great sadness occasioned by what he saw as the disaster to an individual person: the focus of his distress is even more the disastrous end to the prospect of liberation occasioned by the death of 'Jesus of Nazareth, who was a prophet mighty in deed and word before God and all the people, and [whom] our chief priests and leaders handed . . . over to be condemned to death and crucified. But we had hoped that he was the one to redeem Israel' (Luke 24.19–21). Here embedded within an account of a resurrection appearance is the consistent witness of the New Testament that Jesus' death was not self-evidently a rescue. What Cleopas says is, we had expected rescue through this man and all that his death shows is that we were wrong.

THE CHRISTIAN COMMUNITY AND DEATH

If the foreboding apparent in Jesus' facing of his own death is an impression that comes through the gospel record, it is also evident that the earliest Christians also found death a hard reality with which to come to terms. That difficulty was not only the manifestation of ordinary human grief, but represented also the radical disappointment of finding that some of those who had been part of the Christian community had died before their expectation of Christ's return had been fulfilled. If they were offered an account of a Christian hope of a future sharing in the fulfilment of God's promises, it was surely in part because they were seen to need that reassurance, and their grief was found to be an occasion for serious theological reflection on the meaning of death.

> But we do not want you to be uninformed, brothers and sisters, about those who have died, so that you may not grieve as others do who have no hope. For since we believe that Jesus died and rose again, even so, through Jesus, God will bring with him those who have died. For this we declare to you by the word of the Lord, that we who are alive, who are left until the coming of the Lord, will by no means precede those who have died. For the Lord himself, with a cry of command, with the archangel's call and with

the sound of God's trumpet, will descend from heaven, and the dead in Christ will rise first. Then we who are alive, who are left, will be caught up in the clouds together with them to meet the Lord in the air, and so we will be with the Lord forever. Therefore, encourage one another with these words.

1 Thessalonians 4.13–18

We may notice how closely the grief to which the apostle addresses these words corresponds with Martha's words to Jesus after the death of Lazarus: 'Lord, if you had been here, my brother would not have died' (John 11.21, repeated by Mary at John 11.32). If the Lord had returned as the earliest Christians believed he had promised, their brothers and sisters would not have died. And similarly, what the apostle promises is a reflection of what took place at the tomb of Lazarus: a 'word of command', 'Lazarus, come out!' (11.43). The significant point is, however, that clearly for the Thessalonian Christians the deaths of the brothers and sisters was not self-evidently a rescue for them; only a word of gospel could make it so.

Similarly, Paul's lengthy exposition of the hope of future resurrection in 1 Corinthians 15 will certainly have had as one of its aims (at least[4]) an engagement with the grief of the believing community for those of their number who had died, and with their perplexity about how that could have happened in the aftermath of Jesus' resurrection, and in view of his promise to return. The chapter has continued to have such a strong effect in addressing that grief, if not that perplexity, for generations through its use at funerals, that it is hard not to feel that that was a significant part of its intention. The argument may be long and, to our ears, at points strange: but it seeks to connect the experience of death generally, and in the Christian community in particular, with the death of Christ and his resurrection, offering those who grieve for the departed the ringing assurance of its conclusion: 'But thanks

71

be to God who gives us the victory through our Lord Jesus Christ. Therefore, my beloved, be steadfast, immovable, always excelling in the work of the Lord, because you know that in the Lord your labour is not in vain' (1 Corinthians 15.57, 58).

Obviously much more detailed comments could be made about the way in which Paul's argument in 1 Thessalonians and 1 Corinthians seeks to reassure believing, and yet grieving, Christians about the hope of life to come. In particular, I have not so far said anything about the character of the resurrection of Jesus and its relation to Paul's argument. My point here is a more limited one: to make clear that the presence in the New Testament of extended argument about life beyond death, and the lengths to which it was necessary to go in order to reassure Christians about it, is an indication that death was not for them, any more than it is for us, self-evidently some kind of rescue or release.

The presentation of Jesus prior to his death, of the disciples after his death, and then of the New Testament Church later, is of human beings sharing with us the sense of death as a defeat and an ending. Upon reflection, in the light of other convictions and with the teaching of their leaders to guide them, they were able to come to the belief that the death of Christ was a rescue, and that those who died would share in the fruits of that victory. What is more, numerous New Testament passages, and not least the Book of Revelation, offer particular reassurance and encouragement to believers contemplating the deaths of their brothers and sisters as martyrs, associating those deaths in particular with God's ultimate triumph. But the presence and strength of such argument and reassurance are themselves evidence that seeing death, and the death of Christ, as any kind of rescue was not an immediate possibility for our forebears any more than it is for us.

How defeat comes within the New Testament to be seen as victory, and how an ending comes to be accepted as transition to life, is the subject of the next section. But those who grieve for the death of those they love, or who contemplate with apprehension the prospect of their own dying, or who feel a sense of shock and even outrage at the premature deaths of those from whom they had expected great things, need not feel remote from the experience of those who came to faith in the earliest days of Christianity. Like those who marched behind the banners of the miners' lodges, they had every reason to fear that they might only be keeping alive an old tradition, one with no power to liberate them from the difficulties through which they were living, a mere act of remembrance, honourable, even desirable; but not a source of new life for them or transformation for the world. When we ask the question, how did our forebears come to so different a conclusion, willing to confess that, after all, 'Jesus lives' and that his life was available to them and to the world and could command their ultimate allegiance even if it did cost them their lives, we ask it as fellow-seekers after some word, some experience or some reality that might transform defeat into the triumph of life.

IT WAS NECESSARY . . .

Whatever might have been the frequency and manner of Jesus' prediction of his own death, and with whatever detail he foresaw it, the New Testament rests on the conviction that his death was in a far more important sense predicted long before.

> Then [the stranger] said to them, 'Oh, how foolish you are, and how slow of heart to believe all that the prophets have declared! Was it not necessary that the Messiah should suffer these things and then enter into his glory?' Then beginning with Moses and all the prophets, he interpreted to them the things about himself in all the scriptures.
>
> Luke 24.25–7

73

We could imagine a process of reflection on the life of Jesus and on the manner of his death that led to the conclusion that, despite the fact that he endured a violent and unjustified death, he was nevertheless the Messiah. That would have made Jesus' death a dreadful event, an unwarranted and inexplicable interruption of his mission, a tragedy which did not, however, nullify Jesus' status and mission as Christ. Something terrible had gone wrong, but whatever it was did not destroy his claim nor make him any less the one whom it was right to follow.

We could imagine such a process of reflection. It parallels many occasions when we have to cope with unaccountable tragedy, and conclude, despite our perplexity in the face of it, and despite all appearances, that a person had been worthy of our affection or trust, and their untimely death, or whatever form the tragedy takes, was simply that, a tragedy. But the process of reflection with which the New Testament confronts us is quite different: its writers are united in the conviction that as the stranger said to the disciples on their way to Emmaus, and following the emphasis in the Greek, 'surely these things [i.e. the suffering and death about which the disciples were speaking] were what it was necessary for the Messiah to suffer and enter his glory'. The glory of the anointed one was, therefore, not to be seen as having been given by God and simply revealed in the Messiah's life and the victories he won; it was a glory he had to enter precisely by means of what had taken place outside Jerusalem.

The reflection and experience of the earliest Christians, therefore, were not such as to make the cross into something which could be overlooked in an overall estimate of the significance of Christ's life. It led to a fundamental revision of what kind of Christ was to be expected, and by what kind of action, or indeed suffering, he was to be recognized. The fertility of the theological mind of the early Church was intimately related to this profound revision of their inherited patterns of thought. The character of God's agent, the manner of his life, the nature of his triumph and the demands which were made of those who committed themselves to following in his way were all to be discerned in the fact and manner of his dying. So, in a transaction that must have represented hundreds of similar encounters, Philip invites the Ethiopian eunuch also to make the connection between the writings of the prophets, the destiny of the Messiah and his own future life as a believer; he is presented as starting from a position of perplexity simply because nobody has enabled him to make that connection. So Philip ascertains that he is reading from the servant songs of Isaiah, '. . . in his humiliation justice was denied him. Who can describe his generation? For his life is taken away from the earth.' The eunuch's question in response to this passage is precisely, who is this about?

> The eunuch asked Philip, 'About whom, may I ask you, does the prophet say this, about himself or about someone else?' Then Philip began to speak and starting with this scripture, he proclaimed to him the good news about Jesus. As they were going along the road, they came to some water, and the eunuch said, 'Look here is water! What is to prevent me from being baptized?' And Philip said, 'If you believe with all your heart, you may.' And he replied, 'I believe that Jesus Christ is the Son of God.'

> Acts 8.34–7

Such was the revision of thought that lay behind the presentation of the death of Christ in Mark's Gospel.[5] It opens with the proclamation of the imminent kingdom of God, and yet only through the account of misunderstanding, dereliction and death is the Christ able to fulfil his task. Clearly his message needed to be addressed to those for whom an obliteration or at least a partial concealment of the harsh reality of the cross was the right way to proclaim Christ.

But the same reinterpretation appears also in the writings

of Paul. The Epistle to the Galatians makes clear that the
cross is at the centre of the fundamental revision of thought
that the apostle Paul requires of his audience.

> You foolish Galatians! Who has bewitched you? It was
> before your eyes that Jesus Christ was publicly exhibited as
> crucified! The only thing I want to learn from you is this:
> Did you receive the Spirit by doing the works of the law or
> by believing what you heard? . . . Christ redeemed us from
> the curse of the law by becoming a curse for us – for it is
> written, 'Cursed is everyone who hangs on a tree' – in order
> that in Christ Jesus the blessings of Abraham might come
> to the Gentiles, so that we might receive the promise of
> the Spirit through faith.
>
> Galatians 3.1, 2, 13, 14

The cross is central to Paul's theology because it is the
occasion of these most fundamental revisions of thought.
Seeing this death as an occasion of rescue challenges the most
basic assumptions about the character of rescue, and God's
rescuer. It therefore challenges also the means of rescue
commonly sought and proclaimed within human lives and the
life of their society. It requires a change in the most basic
conception of what is to count as the power of God, and therefore as legitimate power for human beings to hold and use:

> For the message about the cross is foolishness to those who
> are perishing, but to us who are being saved it is the power
> of God. For it is written, 'I will destroy the wickedness of
> the wise, and the discernment of the discerning I will
> thwart.' Where is the one who is wise? Where is the scribe?
> Where is the debater of this age? Has not God made foolish
> the wisdom of the world? For since, in the wisdom of God,
> the world did not know God through wisdom, God
> decided, through the foolishness of our proclamation, to
> save those who believe. For Jews demand signs and Greeks
> desire wisdom, but we proclaim Christ crucified, a stum-

bling block to Jews and foolishness to Gentiles, but to those who are called, both Jews and Greeks, Christ the power of God and the wisdom of God. For God's foolishness is wiser than human wisdom, and God's weakness is stronger than human strength.

1 Corinthians 1.18–25

The death of Christ thus becomes not a concession to a tragic reality, in the face of which he is nevertheless able to be acknowledged as Christ, but the centre of the Christian proclamation, and the saving reality which is to shape both Christians' perception of their Lord and the exercise of whatever 'lordship' they may be called to in the life of the world. That is why (to take only one of the recent examples of this century) Barth, Bonhoeffer and their friends saw the *Führerprinzip*, the shape of Hitler's claim to authority, as a fundamental attack not simply on progressive views of democracy but on the heart of the gospel itself.

But if the death of Christ was to change irrevocably and radically believers' conception of the nature of the Christ, and therefore of the pattern of his authority and power, it was also clear that it had to change other concepts at the heart of their religion also. Most radical of all was what was to happen in the Church to belief about the nature of the sacrifice God required, and the priesthood which would have authority to offer it. For the efficacy of Jesus' sacrifice lay not in the ritual cleanness of animal victims but in the love with which he offered himself: his purity came from the power of the divine Spirit.

For if the blood of goats and bulls, with the sprinkling of the ashes of a heifer, sanctifies those who have been defiled so that their flesh is purified, how much more will the blood of Christ, who through the eternal Spirit offered himself without blemish to God, purify our conscience from dead works to worship the living God!

Hebrews 9.13, 14

Together with the revision of the concept of sacrifice in the light of the death of Christ, his death is also seen to change what is involved in representing the people before God. The Levitical priesthood had been required to maintain a distance and a ritual purity in relation to the people, but Jesus' priesthood derives precisely from his being one of them and sharing their burdens. The priesthood of Jesus did not derive from his distance, nor reflect any kind of human status; it was a priesthood that identified itself with the people in trial and suffering.

> Since, then we have a great high priest who has passed through the heaven, Jesus, the Son of God, let us hold fast to our confession. For we do not have a high priest who is unable to sympathize with our weaknesses, but we have one who in every respect has been tested as we are, yet without sin. Let us therefore approach the throne of grace with boldness, so that we may receive mercy and find grace to help in time of need.
>
> Hebrews 4.14–16

Perhaps the supreme expression of the early Christians' conviction that the cross is that which confers and reveals Jesus as the Christ is the Gospel of John. Here the cross is the *exodos*, the departure he is to accomplish, the exaltation by which, when he is lifted up, healing will come to all (3.14) and he will draw all people to himself (12.32). His work is accomplished at the cross (19.30).

So it is that a death which in itself, like every other death, represented an end, a failure, a loss, a tragedy, is turned into a rescue for the world. This radical reformulation of what a death could mean, and how the Messiah was to be understood, acted also to change the perception all believers had of their own death. The beginnings of Christianity amount to nothing less than a radical reconstruction of historic expectations and religious convictions, as well as determining for all Christian believers the nature of the life to which they are called. They brought into being a changed understanding of secular and religious power through what could be said about one person's death and the hopes which it engendered.

Those who continue to declare that the death of Jesus is a saving death are, as we have seen, taking issue with all that suggests that death in general and Jesus' death in particular was not immediately and self-evidently saving. That is why they have to address the question, what was it that enabled the earliest believers to make the connection between death and rescue that has been at the centre of the Christian proclamation from the beginning? That is the question which is to occupy the remainder of this chapter.

TRANSFORMING WORD

The religious history of God's people as the earliest Christians remembered it had always been astonishingly verbal. The astonishment arises simply because the means we take for granted for the production, reproduction and dissemination of words were of course entirely absent from the environment and history that gave us the Bible. Yet the telling, and then the writing, of words constituted a key instrument for the developing and passing on of religious faith. Like all religions, the Hebrew people had built shrines and altars and gathered the people for worship; those acts bore many resemblances to the religious life of the people who surrounded them; but in their words, those they spoke and those they remembered, lay the distinctiveness of their commitment, a distinctiveness reflected in the character of the God whom they served and worshipped.

Words were not, in that sense, only a medium of transmission. They were also part of the message, that which they wished to profess about the God in whom they believed. This was a God who performed verbal acts: God communicated, conversing with chosen intermediaries so that the people would understand. God conversed and argued, so that a relationship full of content could develop. Above all, God gave commands, and those commands were effective; they demanded things of those to whom they were addressed, but even more they called new situations into being.

So the God who did nothing without first revealing it to God's servants the prophets (Amos 3.7) is also the God who issued ten 'words' to Moses on Sinai which were to determine the character of the relationship God had with Israel. This God is also the one who created the heavens and the earth, not by 'making' them but by 'commanding' them into being by the speaking of creative words: 'Let there be light'; and there was light. The emergence of the Old Testament as a body of literature was closely connected with the conviction that the character of God and the ways of God could be put into words, and indeed that words were an indispensable medium for passing on the truth about God and God's character. The earliest Christian community took its origin from a people whose identity was largely given by the scriptural words in which their story, their songs and their laws were recorded. That people believed that its commitment was to a God who was in a very deep sense a God who spoke.

That 'wordiness' is of course a source of immense frustration often to those whose religious sense is related more to what they see and feel and smell than to words. For some, words are often seen as something getting in the way of a spiritual apprehension that is nourished far more by silence, or music or communion with nature. At a human level we need to identify with that frustration and recognize what is often the obstructive nature of much of our verbal expression of religion.

Yet the power of words, and above all of the Word of God, is so crucial a theme in our religious story that it cannot be removed from its central place. Words have the capacity both to hand on stories and to draw boundaries. They are in that sense profoundly and distinctively human; what is more, they were the means of establishing the character of the deity whom the Hebrews and the Christians worshipped, the ways in which that deity differed from others and therefore in which that deity's followers were required to live, ways that were themselves distinctive. Words are the means by which human beings shape their reality, the way in which our experience is organized and conceptualized; what is also clear is that words, and the Word, had a quite central place in the way in which our forebears came to faith.

We have seen that Jesus went to his death having spoken of it to his disciples. We are aware that one of the ways in which the threat which death poses to our sense of meaning can be disarmed is by being spoken of. Most of us can testify of the extent to which our death and that of those dear to us is at least given some shape and meaning if we have time to prepare for it; then the death which by definition cannot be 'fitted in' to the pattern of life is somehow integrated into a relationship, so that a shared past can be remembered and a very different future envisaged. The exchanging of these words does not make the death any less a death or any more wanted; but the words are part of the memory. They reshape it, and place alongside the absolutely unavoidable experience of loss some experience of gift, one that does not in any sense 'compensate' for what is lost, but lives on in parallel with the grief.

At a more public level, we know that meaning is given to the deaths that are died in great and important causes if the martyr goes knowingly to her or his death, and has shared that knowledge more widely. The murder of Martin Luther King was a personal tragedy, as well as a grave setback to the movement which he led; but he had been asked so many times about the possibility of his dying in the cause, and had so often said he was prepared for that fate if it came, that when the assassin's bullet brought him down, that death had already been integrated by Martin Luther King's own words into the pattern of his life and the significance of the struggle. Or we may read the letters and papers which Dietrich Bonhoeffer wrote in his last days and see in them something which gives meaning to an otherwise tragic end: if death cannot in itself be fitted into to a human story, for it simply ends it, it can at least be made part of that story by the words which are spoken about it.

Jesus went to his death having spoken about it. Those preparatory words, we are told, were not understood or accepted by those who heard them. But after all was accomplished, we are told that the disciples remembered what they had heard, and that it started to make sense of it all. So important is this aspect of Jesus' going to his death that by the time of the Gospel of John we are presented not just with hints and premonitions, but with a sustained act of teaching by one about to go to his death, and concerned therefore that those who had been his followers would understand, and so would be able to go with him as far as they could.

So we have the prediction: 'Very truly I tell you, one of you will betray me', the command to Judas to do quickly what he had to do (John 13.21–30), and the directions, 'Little children, I am with you only a little longer; and as I said to the Jews so now I say to you, "Where I am going, you cannot come."' (John 13.33). But these are followed by the long last discourses, all designed to make clear that in some sense the disciples were to be included in the story of his death and what was to follow it. These words and this teaching lead to an account of the passion itself in which the evangelist is able to see the glory already present at the dying; for all has been prepared.

Yet the premonitions and predictions of Jesus in relation to his death were only a beginning, a preparation for a perception of far greater importance. For Jesus was not in the end remembered as a good man who had tragically died but who had prepared his disciples for that death by predicting his fate. That might have done something to assuage their grief, but would not have transformed a basically sad story into the source of a dynamic gospel of rescue for the world. They might have been able, if we may refer back to the story with

which this chapter began, to remember faithfully these traditions, but they would not have been turned into missionaries
of rescue to the ends of the earth. That needed something
more if this death was to become something more.

What the New Testament Church discovered was that
they had a memory of a death which had not merely been
predicted by the dying person; it had in fact been predicted
by God that that was how God's agent was to suffer 'and
enter his glory'. We are told constantly that Jesus died
'according to the scriptures'; that is to say that there were
words about this death, and that they were God's words
about the death of God's agent. What Jesus went to on
Calvary was God's tragedy, something that posed a threat
not simply to Jesus and his life and concerns, but to the very
character of God as God's people had grown to understand it.
And what were needed to enable God's new people to make
sense of that tragedy were not simply human words, but
words which God had given to the people in past ages to
foretell this and give it shape and sense.

It was God's words that gave sense to this otherwise
senseless event: Jesus had been named by God, and the name
had declared his purpose, 'Yahweh-has-saved'. His life had
been lived in accordance with that name; he had lived
according to the word. Then he had died according to the
words which God had spoken to the people, and thus his
death was now part of the story of the God who saves, who
had ordained that death as the way the world was to be
rescued. As Peter's Pentecost sermon has it,

> 'You that are Israelites, listen to what I have to say: Jesus
> of Nazareth, a man attested to you by God with deeds of
> power, wonders, and signs that God did through him
> among you, as you yourselves know – this man, handed
> over to you according to the definite plan and foreknowl-
> edge of God, you crucified and killed by the hands of those
> outside the law.'
>
> Acts 2.22, 23

For that 'definite plan and foreknowledge of God' the early Church was able to find evidence in its constant recourse to the Old Testament Scriptures, the words by which the event of the death of God's agent could be shown to be the world's longed-for rescue. The discovery of that definite plan and foreknowledge was what transformed tragedy into promise and enabled the community of believers to see in that death not merely a tradition worth recalling but the source of life for them all.

Here we come to the limit of the power of words: for there is yet a further question, what it was that enabled the earliest Christian community to return to the Scriptures and find there meaning for this death. And the answer to that has to be some new experience, something that made life in and through death a reality to them, something that could enable them to see in a closed off past the key to a new and open future, and rescue in the midst of disaster. The reason there was and is a Church is more than memory and more than words; it is that the earliest believers encountered an experience which made the words ring true, and so transformed the death which was the theme of this chapter into the promise which is the theme of the next.

5

The Promise

OUR STUDY BEGAN with some of the contemporary issues that arise when we attend to the fact that the Christian proclamation is about a rescue. What are the perils? Which are the false trails that humanity might follow in its search for escape from them? And what are the features of our contemporary situation which present particular challenges to those who seek to commend the Good News of rescue through Jesus Christ in today's world? Those reflections sent us, in chapter 2, back to the New Testament: first, to its witness to Jesus as the named saviour of the world, and therefore to his being the person of destiny, chosen to live out in his day and for his people God's response to their need.

In chapter 3, we saw something of how his life reflected that destiny, and how it was that the rescue he offered was both gift to those who knew themselves to be in need and profound challenge to those whose position in society and guardianship of its traditions were evidently blinding them to the need in which they, and their society, stood. We traced, in the next chapter, something of the inevitability of the death of Jesus in the light of the challenge which his offer of rescue posed to the society and its leadership. That death, in itself as tragic as any death is, was transformed into an instrument of rescue because it had been spoken of in advance, not just in Jesus' own explicit references to it, but (as the Church came later to perceive) in the preparation of God's people by the prophets.

We have sought throughout to use examples to show how the gospel of rescue as it comes to us out of the pages of Scripture can best be perceived if it is connected with some of the situations requiring rescue in our own time. God's rescue, according to the New Testament, is *for all*; in the light of that proclamation of rescue for all we can look at our own lives and the needs of our world afresh. Equally, our reflection on the lives of individuals and societies today can enhance our attentiveness to the New Testament and our openness to the way in which it can address the issues of our lives and of our time and change our perspective on them.

Among such issues of our time, and one that makes the possibility of rescue a highly relevant question, is our concern for the future. The end of the cold war may mean that we have distanced ourselves from a conscious fear of imminent nuclear catastrophe, a sudden end to life as we know it; but human beings are no less dominated by fear for themselves, the species and the universe of which they are part. We are aware of facing issues of life-style, resources and sheer numbers that make God's promise to Noah of a universe in which seedtime and harvest will not fail appear distressingly over-optimistic. We are also aware of challenges to the global economic order that make peace among the nations a terribly fragile hope; we add to that our sense that if one form of international conflict, the cold war, appears to have been brought to an end, there have arisen, in the aftermath of that ending, conflicts of an intractability and a viciousness that make 'peace on earth to all who enjoy God's favour' seem more a wistful longing than a realistic hope. In what way, if at all, can what the New Testament has to say about rescue as God's *promise* relate to that current concern with the fragility of the future and the viability of human hope?

> Jesus' preaching to Israel was the precondition, his death for countless hosts rendered possible, and his parousia will bring into being, the people of God of the New Age, and the Kingdom of God over the whole world.[1]

The New Testament tells us that Jesus was God's way of rescuing us from future condemnation. Other people have averted disasters, shifted entrenched patterns of thought, opened up new possibilities and removed obstacles to human development. They have changed the future in all sorts of ways. We are accustomed to this: politicians and planners, technologists and industrialists are all expected to create for us a new and different future. One major concern of educationalists is to enable students to enter into the world of the future, to adjust to it and to contribute to it. The future is for our making and our improving, so that our children may inherit a world, and if possible a better one than we have known. In a sense human beings share that desire with all creation.

All things living are in search of a better world. Men [sic], animals, plants, even unicellular organisms are constantly active. They are trying to improve their situation, or at least to avoid its deterioration.[2]

We have just alluded to the fact that in our time we approach the future with considerable anxiety, and no great confidence in our ability to secure it. But the Bible too, it is fair to say, is quite sceptical of such futures as we can plan; at points it is even hostile to them. It sees the emerging world, if left to our human devising, as fraught with dangerous possibilities. In particular, the Bible is unromantic about the human capacity to spoil things, and our tendency to act against our own best interests, and even more against the best interests of other people and the creation. If we are to have a future, one that is for our good, it will be the future of God's devising, one that we can come to know not through the predictions we may make or the plans we may hatch, but only as God makes that good future known to us and chooses to give it to us. The images of that future, the one God promises, can be positive and inviting: paths through the wilderness, streams in the desert (Isaiah 43.19) or an end to the grief of the tearful (Revelation 7.17, 21.4). Sometimes the discontinuity with the present age is even more starkly presented:

Since all these things are to be dissolved in this way, what sort of persons ought you to be in leading lives of holiness and godliness, waiting for and hastening the coming of the day of God, because of which the heavens will be set ablaze and dissolved and the elements will melt with fire? But in accordance with his promise, we wait for new heavens and a new earth, where righteousness is at home.

2 Peter 3.11–13

But whatever the picture, God's future is always 'new'.

THE FUTURE AS GIFT

It is for that reason that Jesus' preaching contains over and over again the requirement that we live in a state of constant alertness, as though we did not know the time, because God's future could dawn at any moment. In speaking about this, Jesus does not hesitate to use analogies and experiences that are far from attractive. 'Understand this: if the owner of the house had known in what part of the night the thief was coming, he would have stayed awake and would not have let his house be broken into. Therefore you also must be ready, for the Son of Man is coming at an unexpected hour' (Matthew 24.43).

To act as though you knew God's time-scale exposes you to very considerable risks; while to live in a state of constant readiness is the true wisdom.

'Who then is the faithful and wise slave, whom his master has put in charge of his household, to give the other slaves their allowance of food at the proper time? Blessed is that slave whom his master will find at work when he arrives. Truly I tell you, he will put that one in charge of his possessions. But if that wicked slave says to himself, "My master is delayed," and he begins to beat his fellow slaves, and eats and drinks with drunkards, the master of that slave will come on a day when he does not expect him and at an hour that he does not know. He will cut him in pieces with the hypocrites, where there will be weeping and gnashing of teeth.'

Matthew 24.45–51

What is more, the unknown and imminent character of the coming of God's time leads to an ethic, a demand for kinds of behaviour, which stops us in our tracks. The overriding need for alertness means that we seem to be asked to suspend many of our most cherished understandings of righteous living. The kingdom of heaven, we are told, will be like the situation of the ten bridesmaids of whom only half had enough oil. Clearly the sharing which we might suppose to be the kind thing to do has to take second place in a situation where the bridegroom might arrive at any time and the shared oil might not be sufficient for anyone:

'And while they went to buy the oil, the bridegroom came, and those who were ready went with him into the wedding banquet, and the door was shut. Later the other bridesmaids came also, saying, "Lord, Lord, open to us." But he replied, "Truly I tell you, I do not know you." Keep awake therefore, for you know neither the day nor the hour.'

Matthew 25.10–13

Better not behave as humankind did before the flood, when they ate and drank and made merry and the flood waters came and swept them all away (Matthew 24.37–9).

Likewise proving your oxen, viewing your land, carrying out your conjugal duty, may all be good and right in less urgent days; but this is a time when the banquet is ready and if you do not wish to lose your invitation for ever you must respond now (Matthew 22.2–10). Burying your parent may be a right general obligation for normal times; but in the face of Jesus' call this is not a normal time (Matthew 8.21–2). So we ask ourselves, as we confront this aspect of Jesus' teaching, whether part of our difficulty in meeting the crises of our day lies in our reluctance to be alert enough, to think the radically new thoughts that are required for our rescue.

This strong theme of the imminent and overwhelming future of the kingdom of God has in this century occupied a key place in the developing understanding of the New Testament. Since Albert Schweitzer wrote his *Quest of the Historical Jesus* nobody has been able to ignore that aspect of the teaching of Jesus and the origins of Christianity. For some, like Schweitzer, it threatened the person of Jesus with a profound remoteness from the concerns and preconceptions of our time.

That feeling of remoteness has been dealt with in various ways: Bultmann insisted that only if such ideas of an imminent end of the world and return of Jesus were 'demythologized' could they make any sense at all in our time. On the other hand, the response of theologians such as Wolfhart Pannenberg and Jürgen Moltmann has been to seek to re-establish the biblical categories of promise and fulfilment in our contemporary setting. In so doing they, like the theologians of liberation, have sought to connect themes like judgement to the political struggles of our time. They have seen the promise of God's future as a call to Christians to engage with the needs of society.

> The horizon of expectation within which a Christian doctrine of conduct must be developed is the eschatological horizon of expectation of the kingdom of God, of God's righteousness and peace with a new creation, of God's freedom and humanity for all. This horizon alone, with its formative effect on the present, leads one in missionary hope to oppose and suffer under the inadequacies of the present, bringing one into conflict with the present form of society, and causing one to discover the cross of the present ... Only Christians who no longer understand their eschatological mission as a mission for the future of the world and of humanity can identify their call with the

existing circumstances in the social roles of their callings and be content to fit in with these. But where the call is seen within the horizon of expectation proper to it, there our believing obedience, our discipleship and our love must be understood as creative discipleship and creative love.[3]

Even if, however, we take with full seriousness, as we are bound to do, the power of the note of expectation within the life and teaching of Jesus, and if we interpret his call as one to prepare for God's just future, we are still left with the stark problem, as indeed Schweitzer was, of the failure of that future to come about in the form in which it was expected. Jesus died, as we have seen, in the service of that future, but yet that future, at any rate as his audience expected it, did not happen. At the very beginning of the Christian era believers still waited in hope for Christ's imminent return – but they waited in vain. The expectation has continued to be held within the teaching of the Church, that '[Christ] will come again in his glorious majesty to judge the living and the dead', and particularly among dissenting Christians and persecuted minorities that expectation has sustained their continuing courage and struggle. But the awkward question remains, what are we to make of the conviction that God has promised and will give to humankind the future God intends, in the light of the fact that that future of justice and peace appears as distant as ever?

We should be failing to see the obvious connection with our own experience if we allowed ourselves to see the problem of disappointed expectations as something belonging to the far distant period of the New Testament. Some of the most creative and committed human spirits in every age give themselves to the service of humanity in all kinds of struggles for justice; and for their pains spend years in frustration or even in prison cells as they continue to be disappointed of their hopes, face forces of resistance far more powerful than they had anticipated, and come near to the point of giving up on their task. And when they do find themselves in some sense successful, it is often in ways, and almost always in a time-scale, that they had never anticipated. And what is true of larger public struggles is true also of the course of most people's lives: we plan and work for a future we desire, for ourselves, for our children, for our communities; and in the event the delays are longer and the challenges to our ability to persist more severe than we had ever imagined. The 'successes' when they come are often fleeting, or come in a form quite different from the one we had expected.

In this respect, we can feel much empathy as human beings with the perplexity over the nature and timing of God's final vindication of his Son that is grappled with in the pages of the New Testament. The various writers struggle with the question, have we been given a different future from the one for which we were prepared? And if so what is it, and what has to become of our former expectations?

Yet for all the evident perplexity and struggle, faith was not abandoned. The struggle to understand continued. Behind the persistence of that faith was an experience that captured them and could not be gainsaid: the experience of the resurrection of Jesus Christ, the conviction therefore that the future was after all and despite all appearances his. Because of that experience and that conviction, the question of the future God intended to give continued to be the focus of a profound wrestling. If Jesus lived, and that was the witness of the earliest Christians, then the future was his. Even if we found it immensely difficult to discern how that future accorded with the one God had promised to give, it had to be received as God's gift, and its meaning sought for. The question whether Jesus' predictions of the coming of the kingdom had been from the start misunderstood or perhaps needed in a new situation to be reinterpreted is never finally resolved, and we may say never will be; equally the experience of his continuing life has never been lost and with it the belief remains that God will bring to pass the rescue promised in Jesus.

THE FUTURE OF THE RISEN ONE

Jesus' rescue of his people involved more than a demand that his followers live in a state of alertness in the light of the fact that God's reign might dawn at any moment. After his death, the Church perceived the future as profoundly altered both in its time-scale and in its character. The future was changed in its time-scale, because despite the hope for Christ's return, there developed over time the need to plan for a longer-term future, for institutional stability, and so for the continuing life of the people of God. To that we shall return.

The character of the future was changed in ways that were crucial, and determined at a fundamental level how the gospel came to be understood. In so far as resurrection formed part of the belief of some of Jesus' contemporaries, it was a conviction born in the heat of persecution and martyrdom. The deaths of God's most faithful servants, those who had refused to obey the demands of the heathen, appeared to mean the triumph of God's enemies, and the defeat of God's righteous. How could this be? The conviction that the dead would be raised, and thus that the faithful would be vindicated, was a *theological* conviction, a development of *belief in God*, that allowed God to remain triumphant in the face of what was otherwise disastrous. God's victory was simply, on this understanding, deferred; at some point in the future the dead would be raised for judgement and the wicked for condemnation. We find that belief reflected in the parable of the Rich Man and Lazarus (though not in the conclusion Jesus gives to it), a story which clearly reflects the view that one day the evil order of things would be reversed. That traditional, and harsh, understanding is expressed in Abraham's comment to the rich man in response to his appeal for mercy:

'Child, remember that during your life you received your good things, and Lazarus in like manner evil things; but now he is comforted here, and you are in agony. Besides all this, between you and us a great chasm has been fixed, so that those who might want to pass from here to you cannot do so, and no one can cross from there to us.'

Luke 16.25, 26

This theme of reversal is a development of the confidence of the martyr in God's power and intention to avenge. As one Jewish martyr said to King Antiochus, in the last throes of the agony of torture and martyrdom, 'You accursed wretch, you dismiss us from this present life, but the King of the universe will raise us up to an everlasting renewal of life, because we have died for his laws' (2 Maccabees 7.9).[4] New life, God's future, will be a vindication of God's authority, a seal on God's claim to be the universal king, and at the same time the just reward for faithfulness.

It is not surprising that Jesus' resurrection is therefore appealed to often in the pages of the New Testament as a sign of his vindication. So Peter testifies before the Jerusalem authorities: 'This Jesus is "the stone that was rejected by the builders; it has become the cornerstone." There is salvation in no one else, for there is no other name under heaven given among mortals by which we must be saved' (Acts 4.11, 12). What is more, the resurrection is the sign that the future is indeed to be his; as Paul puts it in his address on the Areopagus, 'God has fixed a day on which he will have the world judged in righteousness by a man whom he has appointed, and of this he has given assurance to all by raising him from the dead' (Acts 17.31). So Jesus has been given his due authority over all things, and that authority sealed by the resurrection: 'God put this power to work in Christ when he raised him from the dead and seated him at his right hand in the heavenly places, far above all rule and authority and power and dominion, and above every name that is named, not only in this age but also in the age to come' (Ephesians 1.20, 21).

So the resurrection of Jesus brings with it the themes of

judgement and reversal, and is the sign that God has vindicated the authority of Jesus. But the resurrection of Jesus brings about another crucial change of perception: the fact that it is Jesus who has been raised changes the character of the future which is his and the judgement which he will apply. For the future is not now a straightforward matter of rewarding the righteous under the Law: because the future belongs to Jesus, one who was crucified outside the Law, the future is one of the inclusion of those outside the Law. That in turn carries with it the central thrust of Paul's proclamation of salvation by the free gift of the grace of God, a dynamic of inclusion which has continued down the ages as the essential character of the future of the risen Christ.

> For this reason it depends on faith, in order that the promise may rest on grace and be guaranteed to all his descendants, not only to the adherents of the law, but also to those who share the faith of Abraham (for he is the father of all of us, as it is written 'I have made you the father of many nations') – in the presence of the God in whom he believed, who gives life to the dead and calls into existence the things that do not exist . . . No distrust made him waver concerning the promise of God, but he grew strong in his faith as he gave glory to God, being fully convinced that God was able to do what he had promised.
>
> Romans 4.16–18, 20–21

This new future created by grace was the future of Jesus because it continued, in the new situation of the early Church, the dynamic of his commitment to the rescue of the lost. 'Yahweh has saved' – and the Lord continues to save, 'not the righteous but sinners'. So the continuing future of the risen Christ is one in which God's promise of rescue extends to all those who are outcast from the Covenant. This dynamic of inclusion which had led, as we have seen, to the inevitability of Jesus' death became known in the dynamic of his new life, a life which continued the concern for the lost which had been his mission both in his life and in his death.

It was this perceived dynamic of rescue, the inclusion of the excluded, which enabled Paul to struggle with understanding God's purpose in what must have been, for him as well as for his hearers, the most difficult of all features of their situation with which to come to terms, the rejection (as they saw it) of Jesus the Messiah by God's own people. How is God's inclusive purpose to be understood in such a context? Could God now, in the process of including the Gentiles, reject the chosen people? And if so, could that not be a source of pride and boasting among new converts as they observed Christ's rejection by the Jews? Paul is determined to resist this implication, convinced that God's will is to include all. In the part of the Epistle to the Romans which is devoted to this matter, you can hear him, as it were, torn apart by the dilemma with which he is faced, but yet insisting that rejection cannot be God's ultimate purpose.

> And even those of Israel, if they do not persist in unbelief, will be grafted in, for God has the power to graft them in again. For if you have been cut from what is by nature a wild olive tree and grafted, contrary to nature, into a cultivated olive tree, how much more will these natural branches be grafted back into their own olive tree. So that you may not claim to be wiser than you are, brothers and sisters, I want you to understand this mystery: a hardening has come upon part of Israel until the full number of the Gentiles has come in. And so all Israel will be saved . . . Just as you were once disobedient to God but have now received mercy because of their disobedience, so they have now been disobedient in order that, by the mercy shown to you, they too may now receive mercy. For God has imprisoned all in disobedience, so that he may be merciful to all.
>
> Romans 11.23–6, 30–2

Thus what God intends is a process by which all can be

included on the basis of grace and none may claim their inclusion to be due to their kinship, their achievement of righteousness or their membership of the Covenant, Old or New. Such is God's continuing of Jesus' work of rescuing the excluded: as Paul exclaims, 'O the depth of the riches and wisdom and knowledge of God! How unsearchable are his judgements, and how inscrutable his ways!' (11.33).

A FUTURE TO PLAN AND TO GUARD

It takes very little reflection to see just how difficult it is to proclaim a gospel of rescue as it has just been described. Such a gospel amounts to the proclamation of continuous revolution. That phrase belongs most particularly to the recent history of China, and we know how very easily such revolutions produce their own outcasts and discard the promised programme of inclusion and the rights of persons. We know that at the most basic level it is very difficult to retain in government what you profess in opposition, how hard it will be, for example, for a newly elected, multi-ethnic administration in South Africa to avoid the use of all the mechanisms of state security and repression which were once used to defend apartheid, given the pressures that will surely surface in the new South Africa.

For inclusion, a word that has been repeatedly used here to describe the way in which the gospel of rescue proved stronger than the boundaries which might have limited its scope, contains possibilities of misunderstanding which are themselves not new. It is easy to convey the impression that the breaking open, through the action of God in Jesus, of boundaries that had previously excluded those classed as 'sinners' and those known as 'Gentiles' meant also the breaking down of all boundaries of belief and behaviour. Talk of 'all may come' leads quickly to speaking as though 'anything goes'. We know that the gospel of rescue includes people within the community of grace; but it also includes them within the community which seeks to live out the demands of the gospel and to hand on faithfully the message of Jesus. The gospel of inclusion may be one of overflowing generosity; it is also one of overwhelming demand, and holding these two aspects together is no easy matter.

It is this double edge to inclusion that accounts for our common experience that often society's victims, be they the victims of oppression or sickness, can be quite as resistant to any change in their situation, even the possibility of what might be a change for the better, as are those who may see their power or position threatened. For those at the margin know well that any call to be included is also a call to responsibility.[5] It demands an end to the excuse that powerlessness often offers. 'Do you want to be made well?' we hear Jesus asking the man lying at the pool by the Sheep Gate in Jerusalem (John 5.6) – and it is a real question which has real echoes in the lives of people in all sorts of situations of disadvantage. They know instinctively what many who have experienced healing or who have known nothing but security or privilege easily forget: that inclusion is no soft option, but a call to responsibility.

That makes it not in the least surprising how quickly the early Church is involved in internal conflict about how such an inclusive gospel is to be preached and safeguarded. On the one hand we have already seen how those who had inherited an understanding of the nature of God's people from their formation as Jews believed that any modification of the requirements of the Law would jeopardize the fulfilment of God's purpose. On the other hand we see clear signs, for example in the churches to which the Epistles to the Corinthians were addressed, of the emergence of an ecstatic sense that all was now fulfilled and complete freedom from law of any kind was to be encouraged.

To the former, Paul appears as the agent of an almost anarchic freedom; to the latter he has to appear as exerting an almost authoritarian control as he insists on the priority of respect for authority and mutual regard. On the one hand he is presenting the Christian life as founded on God's boundless mercy, on a gracious act that has brought about a community of grace in which all can be included. On the other hand he calls for a disciplined waiting for the future yet to be disclosed, and an approach to each other by members of the Christian community that acknowledges that whatever are the gifts of the Spirit we now possess, none is worth anything unless we also acknowledge our incompleteness. Like children we have not yet entered our full inheritance, and therefore those who make large claims that they have entered the totality of the future which belongs to Jesus need to be aware that much of what they now boast of is only temporary.

> Love never ends. But as for prophecies, they will come to an end; as for tongues, they will cease; as for knowledge, it will come to an end. For we know only in part, and we prophesy only in part; but when the complete comes, the partial will come to an end. When I was a child, I spoke like a child, I thought like a child, I reasoned like a child; when I became an adult, I put an end to childish ways. For now we see in a mirror, dimly, but then we will see face to face. Now I know only in part; then I will know fully, even as I have been fully known.
>
> 1 Corinthians 13.8–12

Such exhortations to love and forbearance, however, are not all that has to be done to guard the future which belongs to Jesus. We can see at all sorts of points the vulnerability of the gospel to false interpretation, and the need to limit debate within the bounds approved by those in positions of leadership. If the future is to belong to Jesus, not all opinions and directions can be approved. As the life of the early Church develops, so also does a sense of threat; if the gospel of rescue for all is to be preached, then it too seems to need to be rescued from those who are thought to be adapting it to their own purposes.

In the presence of God and of Christ Jesus, who is to judge the living and the dead, and in view of his appearing and his kingdom, I solemnly urge you: proclaim the message; be persistent whether the time is favourable or unfavourable; convince, rebuke, and encourage, with the utmost patience in teaching. For the time is coming when people will not put up with sound doctrine, but having itching ears, they will accumulate for themselves teachers to suit their own desires, and will turn away from listening to the truth and wander away to myths.

2 Timothy 4.1–4

The pages of the New Testament present examples of every kind of option in the struggle to guard the future which belongs to Jesus, on the one hand, in its essential freedom, and on the other to provide the disciplined framework to guard it from fatal distortion. Sometimes it seems we are in the presence of a community oscillating between extreme positions; on other occasions, as for example in the outcome of the Council of Jerusalem in Acts 15, we seem to be in the presence of the spirit of compromise, the attempt to resolve the conflict of extremes in a way which will guard the unity of the fellowship. And that itself becomes a key component of the future which belongs to Jesus, a community which lives out its calling to be his body. Without that the future which belongs to Jesus cannot be guarded; but the appeal for the unity of spirit in the bonds of peace is also an instrument of control, a limit to the freedom of the spirit, an excluding tendency which itself at times needed resisting in the interests of a truth which could not forever be found in the realm of compromise.[6]

Such then is the New Testament's struggle over the character of Jesus' rescue of the future. He rescued it from false directions; and he rescued it also from the apparent safety of exclusiveness. He was found to have rescued it from an ecstasy of fulfilment which sacrificed all the necessary fabric of community for the joy of being in the Spirit, and at the same time from the rigid framework of a law which could come to hold God's future at bay. Such is the extremity of ambivalence to which the New Testament exposes us time and again. And with that exposure comes the question, how is that rescue to be lived and guarded in our day? What are the directions in which our survey of the New Testament material propels us?

THE PRACTICE OF PROMISE

The tragedy of Jesus' death was turned into the promise of rescue for all, and for the world which was otherwise destined for disaster. If we are to be faithful to our reading of the New Testament witness, we have to say that the passion of Jesus was 'turned into' the promise of rescue, not simply that it was 'understood' in that new way. The emergence of that promise was not simply the result of theological reflection, or the recycling of the memories of Jesus' life and suffering by people who, in some remarkable way, came to terms with their grief. Jesus' risen life did indeed manifest itself in the faith of the early Christian community, but his resurrection cannot be reduced to the appearance of that faith. What the early Church found present within it was not just *faith in* Jesus, but *the life of* Jesus, himself continuing 'to be and to operate';[7] in their experience, 'Yahweh saves'.

Yet the basis of this experience included the components of the life of the early Church, seen to be continuous with the action, preaching, living and dying of Jesus; it was Jesus who had been raised to life, and not another. So the gospel of God's rescue as it was preached, promised and practised in Jesus' life was also experienced in the life of the Church, and not just hoped for. Healing, the bringing into being of God's promise of rescue for individuals and communities, was a feature of their life together. So was prophecy, the declaring of God's judgement and purpose in the face of injustice and wickedness, as they found at the heart of their life together the fulfilment of the prophecies of former years, and saw in them also what God had been about in Jesus.

> In the last days it will be, God declares, that I will pour out my Spirit on all flesh, and your sons and your daughters shall prophesy, and your young men shall see visions, and your old men shall dream dreams. Even upon my slaves, both men and women, in those days I will pour out my Spirit, and they shall prophesy. And I will show portents in the heaven above and signs on the earth below, blood, and fire, and smoky mist. The sun shall be turned to darkness and the moon to blood, before the coming of the Lord's great and glorious day. Then everyone who calls on the name of the Lord shall be saved.
>
> Joel 2.28–32, quoted Acts 2.17–21

That promise of universal rescue was the day-to-day experience of the earliest believers, who found within their community, as we have seen, the experience of the redemption of the outcast, the bringing near of those who had been far off (Ephesians 2.13). That experience was to be not something they had wanted, planned and executed for themselves, but the *gift* of the future that had been promised, and which Jesus had bestowed by his life and his death. For that day-to-day experience only one explanation could do justice, namely that Jesus who had been dead was in truth alive, his appearance to those who had seen him now confirmed and given meaning by the reality of promise fulfilled. His life had been what inaugurated that new future and made it possible for others to enter into it: he was both *archēgos*, the pioneer and leader of the community of faith, and would be also the *teleiōtēs*, the one who would bring it to perfection, the one who had practised the life of promise and who was therefore the source of promise to all who believed. 'Let us run with patience the race that is set before us, looking to Jesus the pioneer and perfecter of our faith, who for the sake of the joy that was set before him endured the cross, disregarding its shame, and has taken his seat at the right hand of the throne of God' (Hebrews 12.1, 2).

Faith in Jesus, therefore, required the continued practice of the life of promise, the exhibiting within the life of the believing community of the key components of Jesus' own life. So, as the Epistle to the Hebrews spells it out, since Jesus 'suffered outside the city gate in order to sanctify the people by his own blood', that is where the believer must go to him, 'outside the camp, bearing the abuse he endured'. As he was cast out of his own city, so here 'we have no lasting city, but we are looking for the city that is to come' (13.12–14). Similarly, the life of discipline, generosity and hospitality is enjoined because to Jesus has been given the shaping of the community of faith and the life of the world, because God has vindicated the life he lived and the death he died. 'Now may the God of peace, who brought back from the dead our Lord Jesus, the great shepherd of the sheep, by the blood of the eternal covenant, make you complete in everything good, so that you may do his will, working among us that which is pleasing in his sight' (Hebrews 13.20–1).

The practice of the promise of rescue is what is asked for from the Christian community; it includes the experience of what is to come, and a continued, active, waiting for it. It is characteristic of that practice that it involves numerous paradoxes, but without embracing those paradoxes the Church either degenerates into a community of mere longing, or loses the sense of longing in a belief that all is fulfilled. The risks of those extremes were well known to the New Testament community.

ALL IS ACHIEVED

The experience of the risen life of Christ within the community of faith was clearly one of tremendous power. The experience of forgiveness, of the end of alienation and of membership of the community of the new covenant was bound to lead in many cases to an outburst of spiritual fervour, and the conviction that heaven could be within the grasp of all who believed. Rescue had happened; all were saved. The Christian faith could then be the successful mystery cult in a world where a vast appetite existed for true knowledge and spiritual experience. A church in which that was true could be a community full of vitality, of spiritual gifts and an overwhelming sense of living in the age to come. But it could also turn into an anarchic sect, torn by factionalism as each individual and group claimed to have direct access to life in the Spirit, and were determined upon the exclusion of those from whom they differed. How often has the equivalent of this error been repeated, when those who have been successful in one stage of a struggle lose their hold on the awareness of how much is yet to be achieved.

To such communities, a word of caution and discipline had to be spoken, as it has often had to be since. As we have already seen in Paul's writing to the Corinthians, he insists that they continue to live as those who know that the fullness of Christ's victory has yet to be experienced. In attending to those words of warning, the early Church would have been able to tap into some of the most significant teaching of Jesus about the kingdom of God. For example, the parable of the Sower with its account of the immense crop that would come from God's overflowing generosity was also able to speak different lessons at different times to churches with different needs. It could be heard speaking to those whose response lacked depth, who moved too fast into the ecstasy of fulfilment:

> The sower sows the word. These are the ones on the path where the word is sown: when they hear, Satan immediately comes and takes away the word that is sown in them. And these are the ones sown on rocky ground: when they hear the word, they immediately receive it with joy. But they have no root, and endure only for a while; then, when

trouble or persecution arises on account of the word, immediately they fall away.

Mark 4.14–17

Similarly, the tendency to exclusiveness among those captivated by the new life in Christ seemed to be addressed by an account of God's activity which required human beings to behave with patience, not rushing to judgement: the owner of the wheatfield who finds weeds sown among the wheat seems to be speaking with the voice of a God who alone knows the times and seasons, as well as with the sternness of an apostle seeking to restrain an over-zealous community. He says to those eager to remove the weeds: 'No; for in gathering the weeds you would uproot the wheat along with them. Let both of them grow together until the harvest' (Matthew 13.29, 30).

And most powerfully of all, the Church had to be recalled to the fact that Christ was not to be assumed to be most of all where he was named and known, but would appear for judgement among those who were the least, and would be worshipped most truly by those who, without knowing whom they were serving, nevertheless were honouring Christ:

> 'Then the righteous will answer him, "Lord, when was it that we saw you hungry and gave you food, or thirsty and gave you something to drink? And when was it that we saw you a stranger and welcomed you, or naked and gave you clothing? And when was it that we saw you sick or in prison and visited you?" And he will answer them, "Truly I tell you, just as you did it to one of the least of these who are members of my family, you did it to me."'

Matthew 25.37–40

NOURISHMENT IN HOPE
The practice of promise also means being aware of the need

for continual nourishment and refreshment in the life of Christ. A key element of that practice is therefore the emergence of a sacramental theology that requires an engagement over time with the life of Christ as a means of grace and of being sustained in hope. Paul's handing on of the eucharistic tradition as part of his teaching to the Corinthian church is particularly significant for the way in which, having recounted the words of Christ on the night of his betrayal, he concludes: 'For as often as you eat this bread and drink the cup, you proclaim the Lord's death until he comes' (1 Corinthians 11.26). The full rescue of the world is yet to come, and the community of faith must not imagine it can do without the nourishment it requires to prepare for it. Paul's words pick up the dimension of hope and patience contained in the concluding words of Jesus in Mark's account of the last supper, 'Truly I tell you, I will never again drink of the fruit of the vine until that day when I drink it new in the kingdom of God' (Mark 13.25).

This sense of a community nourishing itself as it looks forward in hope to the fulfilment of the promises of Christ is developed most powerfully in St John.[8] Its presence there is particularly significant in a Gospel which contains no account of actions with bread and wine at the last supper, but where the feeding of the multitude is a foretaste of the kingdom of God and is the occasion for a very strong declaration about the importance of being nourished in hope:

> Jesus said to them, 'Very truly, I tell you, unless you eat the flesh of the Son of Man and drink his blood, you have no life in you. Those who eat my flesh and drink my blood have eternal life, and I will raise them up at the last day; for my flesh is true food and my blood is true drink. Those who eat my flesh and drink my blood abide in me, and I in them. Just as the living Father sent me, and I live because of the Father, so whoever eats me will live because of me. This is the bread that came down from heaven, not like

that which your ancestors ate, and they died. But the one
who eats this bread will live forever.

John 6.53–8

Here we can see, incidentally, how important it is to be
clear that St John does not abandon the idea of a future hope,
yet to be fulfilled, in favour of a Christ who has fulfilled all
things already. Indeed Jesus already is the resurrection and
the life (11.25), but the believer has yet to come to that
fulfilment, and to do so requires a constant accompanying of
Christ, for life is ours still only in hope. As Barrett puts it,

> There is no feeding on the flesh of the Son of man, whether
> by mystical union or in the eucharist, that makes the
> believer an autonomous, self-sufficient source of life. At the
> last day, and every day, he will live only if he is raised up.
> The eschatological element in the Fourth Gospel is not
> accidental; it is fundamental. To have abandoned it would
> have been to abandon the biblical framework of primitive
> Christianity, and to run all the risks to which a purely
> metaphysical Christianity, divorced from history, is ex-
> posed. The dangers of mysticism, perfectionism, and antino-
> mianism are, in this gospel, held in check by the constraint
> of the primitive Christian eschatology, which is a constant
> reminder that the church lives by faith, not by sight, and
> that it is saved in hope.[9]

The firmness of that message, reinforced in the New
Testament in such a variety of ways as we have seen, is a
crucial antidote to all religious tendencies to assert that all is
fulfilled, an assertion that usually has the effect of justifying
the believer's own existing way of life or spiritual perception.
It appears also as justification for the institutional self-
assertion of ecclesiastical organizations which easily claim to
possess within their own structures the fullness of Christ's
offer of rescue for the world.

But the New Testament does not allow us to rest in such a

confident self-assertion. It speaks too much of a Christ who comes to undermine such certainties with the uncertainty he requires us to have about God's time-scale and our own tendency to judge. He insists that he will come at unexpected times for which we have to be alert, and in unknown guises, which will test our openness to him in the person of the least of the brothers and sisters.

Nor does it allow us to rest in the assumption that those who have seen their ideas or their strength rewarded with power are thereby to be respected as those to whom we should give our allegiance, whether they wear appropriate religious designations or not; for Jesus spoke truth to power, and does so still. He does so because through him Yahweh saves, and before that rescue the world and its structures need to tremble. We are not allowed, either, to construct systems that claim to hold for certain the presence of Christ for all time, because the one whose death brought about the rending of the veil of the temple and the breaking down of the dividing wall of partition has not guaranteed a share of his inheritance to people merely because they address him appropriately.

'You shall call his name Jesus, for he shall rescue his people from their sins': with this naming we began. It was a name that expressed a call to operate, to live and to die in certain ways and for certain reasons, which we have sought to examine. That Jesus lived, and died, in accordance with that name and that call is what the early Church remembered, and found continually present as his life burst out in their communities, still speaking truth to power, still including the excluded, still calling people to live in the hope of a world that would be rescued from futility in order to enter God's children's glorious liberty.

That is the promise which is held out by that name, as it has been lived and died and as it still has power to kindle hope and to draw from those who are called by it the ability to live lives of grace which, though far from what they are intended to become, still show the marks of the rescue which has been offered to them in Christ. For them, and for the Church as a body, what is offered is not a set of human structures in which they might permanently place their hope, but the continued presence of a life that calls into being things which are not yet. It is a life that will not be constrained by what we have learned so far or what we have managed to create up to now.

'For the promise is for you, for your children, and for all who are far away, everyone whom the Lord will call to him' (Acts 2.39).

WHO NEEDS RESCUE?

This is the question with which this book began, and to which we must now return. Our attention to the New Testament in the light of issues in our own day has revealed that the question goes deeper than we might at first have recognized or indeed wished. For if the question is asked in the assurance that we know the answer, the New Testament, because it contains so many examples of people who thought they did also, unnerves us by turning the question back on us and requiring us to ask it again.

If we suppose, for example, that those in need of rescue are other than ourselves, those whom we may think of as in some way weak or in need, we are likely to hear ourselves asked whether we ourselves need rescue from our self-assurance, or even from our blindness to our own complicity in what makes others needy. That was the uncomfortable experience of those who watched Jesus heal and did not relish the challenges contained in Jesus' healings to those who saw no need of any physician. We might ask, as an instance from our own day, 'Who needs rescue from racism?', and we might be clear at once that the answer is that those on the receiving end of discrimination are those who need that rescue. But a moment's reflection makes clear that the victims of that discrimination present a question and a challenge to the whole of society, and reveal its deep need of rescue from the processes that lead to discrimination. So when Richard Holloway uses as a book title the question, 'Who needs feminism?', the obvious initial answer, that women do, comes quickly to appear all too superficial; certainly the book shows that men need that rescue at least as much.[10] Of course the 'rescue' needed by the marginalized is not the same as that needed by those who are accomplices in causing them to be marginalized: but the question, 'Who needs rescue?' is nevertheless one that turns back on those who assume too quickly that they know it is others rather than themselves.

We may on the other hand assume that the answer to the question, 'Who needs rescue?' is 'I do.' Like the paralysed man and his friends we may be sure of our presenting problem and want to demand that it be addressed. In that case, again, the question may return to us, demanding a deeper look at our own needs, asking that we address them at their roots. We may also be far from willing to enter into the life of responsibility which the gift of rescue will ask of us. In that case the question will also turn itself back to us: how much do you want this rescue for which you ask, and what cost are you willing to bear to forgo whatever advantage you have sought to gain from being a victim?

The question 'Who needs rescue?' can also be asked cynically or angrily by those sure that all is well, that demands for action are misplaced or self-serving. Such responses have been made as an excuse for resistance to necessary change ever since Pharaoh's heart was hardened against the cry of the Hebrew slaves, and will doubtless continue to be. To those who ask the question in that tone of voice, the question returns with persistence: are you sure? And is your assurance the product of your determination not to see or not to hear?

Yet others may say, 'Who needs rescue?' because they are sure that they have been rescued, that therefore they have no need of it themselves. Such assurance is also, as we have seen, well known to the writers of the New Testament, and they well know how damaging its consequences can be. Rescue we may have been given; but the working out of it and the continuing need for it remain part of our life, the experience of all those who know that in its fullness rescue belongs still in the realm of promise, of that for which we are to wait and to long.

So the question with which we began is reinforced rather than resolved by our exploration. It involves us in a deeper attentiveness to our own and others' needs, as well as to the needs of the society of which we are part. At the same time, through the dialogue which it has required us to have with the New Testament, it has put us into closer touch with the range, the scope and the depth of what God offers. In a society that operates largely on non-religious assumptions, the question of rescue may, at first, not seem the one that most needs asking; and to those who ask it, the New Testament's offer may not instantly seem to meet all the manifold needs of rescue expressed in the world we now inhabit. But what appears in the end is that it asks a deeper question and offers a more radical challenge than at first we supposed. It asks now as it asked then that human beings acknowledge, in whatever situation they occupy, the demand of the judgement they face and the generosity of the gift they are offered.

NOTES

Chapter 1

1 John V. Taylor, *The Christlike God* (SCM Press 1994), p. 76.

Chapter 2

1 Walter Brueggemann, *The Prophetic Imagination* (Fortress Press 1978), p. 25.
2 See the articles on 'Name' (Vol. 3, pp. 500–8) and 'God, Names of' (Vol. 2, pp. 407–17) in *Interpreter's Dictionary of the Bible* (Abingdon Press 1962); also the article on 'Names of God' in *Anchor Bible Dictionary*, Vol. 4, pp. 1001ff.
3 Edward Schillebeeckx, *Jesus* (English edition, Collins 1974), p. 17.
4 Professor Richard Siebeck, quoted in Paul Tournier, *What's In a Name?* (English edition, SCM Press 1975).
5 cf. C. F. Evans, *St Luke* (SCM Press 1990), p. 386. G. B. Caird suggests the man's distress may have arisen from some traumatic experience associated with the Roman occupation (*The Gospel of St Luke* (Penguin Books, 1963)), while A. R. C. Leaney speaks of the 'loss of the unity of the man's personality' (*Commentary on the Gospel according to St Luke* (A. & C. Black 1958)); but this uncertainty about the nature of the man's illness simply confirms its 'namelessness'.
6 Beatrix Campbell, *Goliath* (Methuen 1993), p. 95.
7 Brueggemann, *The Prophetic Imagination*, p. 24.

Chapter 3

1 Jeanie Wylie-Kellermann, 'Rejecting "Normalcy"' (*The Witness*, June 1994).
2 Nancy Westerfield, 'Reserved for the Handicapped' (*The Witness*, June 1994).
3 cf. William Countryman, *Dirt, Greed and Sex*. Also, Walter

Wink, 'The Bible and Exclusion, Bias and Prejudice' (*The Witness*, June 1994).

4 See Evans, *St Luke*, p. 708.

5 I am indebted to the very full interpretation of this episode in Sandra M. Schneiders, *The Revelatory Text* (Harper 1991), ch. 7.

6 I have written more fully about the connections between private and public hurt and their overcoming in *Liberating God: Private Care and Public Struggle* (SPCK 1983), now available as *A World Come of Age* (Cowley Press 1983).

Chapter 4

1 See Huw Beynon, *Masters and Servants: Class and Patronage in the Making of a Labour Organization* (Rivers Oram 1994).

2 See Evans, *St Luke*, p. 540.

3 Though subsequently some have found Barabbas an important figure with which to identify. Cf. Per Lagerkvist's novel, *Barabbas* (1952).

4 The debate about the interpretation of this chapter continues; for an outline of some of its possible aims and the context in which it was written, in relation to belief in the resurrection, see my *Look for the Living* (SCM Press 1976).

5 See for example Morna D. Hooker, *The Message of Mark* (Epworth Press 1983), ch. 7.

Chapter 5

1 J. Jeremias, *Jesus' Promise to the Nations* (SCM Press 1956), p. 73.

2 K. R. Popper, *In Search of a Better World* (Routledge 1992), p. 1.

3 J. Moltmann, *Theology of Hope* (SCM Press 1967), p. 334.

4 I discussed some of this more fully in my *Look for the Living*.

5 See the section on 'The Demands of a Rescue' in Taylor, *The Christlike God*, pp. 83ff.

6 For a very full, though somewhat suspicious, discussion of this tension, see Graham Shaw, *The Cost of Authority: Manipulation and Freedom in the New Testament* (SCM Press 1983).

7 The phrase is from C. F. Evans, *Resurrection and the New Testament* (SCM Press 1970), p. 128.

8 See Stephen Barton, *The Spirituality of the Gospels* (SPCK 1992), pp. 123f.

9 C. K. Barrett, *The Gospel According to St John* (SPCK 1978), pp. 69f.

10 Richard Holloway, *Who Needs Feminism? Male Responses to Sexism in the Church* (SPCK 1991).